MW01601521

GET IE
Speaking Practice – Book 1

Our strategies for success in the IELTS speaking test
With
Twenty complete practice tests
And
**Twenty complete examples of band 9 candidates
taking the practice tests**

Books In This Series:
Book 1 – ISBN 979-8877037113
Book 2 - ISBN 979-8335257527

This completely updated and expanded 2024 paperback edition is
published by
Cambridge IELTS Consultants
Cambridge, United Kingdom

Series Editor: Peter Swires

Copyright © Cambridge IELTS Consultants and Peter Swires 2024

CONTENTS

Editor's Introduction

Many people taking the IELTS exam don't prepare fully for the speaking test. This is unfortunate, because with help (and lots of practice) you can learn some very powerful ways to get the best possible band score, even if your English has some errors or your vocabulary is limited.

In our years of experience preparing candidates for the IELTS exam, we have found that people can improve their band score by up to three levels just by improving their test strategies. This book shows you our proven strategies for each part of the speaking test, plus twenty complete speaking tests for you to apply these methods. Each practice test also has a complete transcript example of a candidate giving answers at a band 9 standard, so you can see the methods in action. By learning our methods and using these practice tests to develop your skills, you will have the best possible chance of doing well in your speaking test.

This is Book 1 in our series on IELTS speaking. Book 2 has a further twenty practice tests and transcripts to develop your skills even further, but it's best to start right here at Book 1 to get a complete introduction to our methods.

We wish you the very best for your IELTS test, and of course for all your future plans.

Peter Swires
Cambridge IELTS Consultants

cambridgeielts@outlook.com

Frequently Asked Questions About the IELTS Speaking Test

What happens in the Speaking Test?

The speaking test lasts roughly eleven minutes, and has three parts. Strategies for each part are explained fully in this book. You (the candidate) will enter a room where an examiner is sitting at a table; the candidate and the examiner are the only people in the room. Your conversation with the examiner is recorded digitally in order to verify the grade that the examiner gives you. The examiner will check your ID and provide you with paper and a pencil to make notes during Part 2 of the test.

What happens in Part 1?

The examiner will ask you a series of questions about some part of your life, for example your home country, your friends or your plans for study and work.

What happens in Part 2?

The examiner gives you a topic to talk about, related to something in your past or present life. You have one minute to prepare, and then you need to speak on the topic for between one and two minutes.

What happens in Part 3?

The examiner will discuss with you a general topic which is related to the personal topic you spoke about in Part 2. For example, if in Part 2 you spoke for two minutes about a city that you know, Part 3 might be a discussion about city life generally.

How does the examiner mark my speaking?

The examiner is looking for full answers to the questions asked, using a wide range of vocabulary and grammatical structures. The examiner will expect your answers to be relevant, well-structured and accurate. This is why you need to use the strategies we teach in this book. The examiner will make notes on a pad while you are speaking; don't try to see what the examiner is writing!

What are the examiners like as people?

IELTS examiners are trained to be friendly, professional and to make you feel comfortable. They are used to candidates being slightly nervous, and they will try to help you relax. You should try to build a professional rapport with the examiner as soon as you meet. You should smile, say *'Nice to meet you'* and offer to shake the examiner's hand if your culture allows this. You should sit at the table in a professional way, as if you were at a seminar or a meeting, placing your hands in view and leaning slightly forward to maintain eye contact. This might be different from your personal style, but it will show the examiner that you are alert and interested in the test.

How fast should I speak?

Try to speak at a normal professional speed. 'Professional' in this context means the way you would speak in a seminar or business meeting in an English-speaking situation. Please note that this may be slower or faster than the speed you naturally speak when talking in your mother tongue language. You should not get excited or emotional while speaking, and don't try to make jokes about anything in the test.

Should I speak in a very formal or academic way?

No, this is not necessary. Candidates sometimes think that they need to speak in the same way as they would write in the IELTS writing test part two, for example by using formal words such as *'therefore'* and *'nevertheless.'* In the speaking test, this is optional, but not necessary. It's more important to use the most advanced and natural English that you can, and organise your answers in the way we explain in this book.

I speak English with quite a strong accent. Is this a problem?

This is not normally a problem. The examiner will not reduce your marks because of an accent, unless your pronunciation makes it difficult to understand the content of what you're saying.

I make some grammatical mistakes when I speak English. Is this a problem?

If you make a few mistakes which don't stop the examiner understanding you, this is not a major problem. We have seen many cases of candidates who have a strong accent and who make some small grammatical mistakes, who still go on to achieve band 8 or 9 in IELTS Speaking. A problem only arises if your errors stop the examiner from understanding what you mean.

Let's begin now by studying the best methods for Part 1 of the test. If you need a dictionary while reading, we recommend the free 'Cambridge Dictionaries Online' from Cambridge University Press.

***

Strategies For Part 1 Of the Speaking Test

In Part 1 (which lasts roughly three to four minutes) the examiner asks you a series of questions about your life and/or your current situation. These questions may be on a single topic (e.g. your leisure interests) or on a variety of topics (e.g. your leisure interests, your friends and your living accommodation.)

Here is an example of three typical Part 1 questions, and three answers from a candidate who would get a medium score (around band 5 or 6.)

Examiner: Let's talk about your home country. What's the climate like?

Candidate: **It's hot most of the time. Sometimes there is rain.**

Thank you. What are the main industries?

Making cars and buses. And there are many factories which make plastic things.

I see. And what are the main festivals?

What does 'festival' mean?

It means a special time when communities and families celebrate something.

Oh, ok. Well, our big festival is in summer.

I see.

Please note that the answers from this candidate do not contain any grammatical mistakes. Also, it is not a problem that the candidate asked for an explanation of the word *'festival.'* The reason that the mark would be quite low is because the information that the candidate provided was too basic, and the candidate did not expand on his initial comment.

How To Answer the Part 1 Questions Using a Two-step Process

Now here is an example of the same questions from the same examiner to a different candidate. This candidate would receive a Band 9 score for this part of the test.

Examiner: Let's talk about your home country. What's the climate like?

Candidate: **It's generally hot and humid, although it rains heavily in October. This has a big impact on our way of life and our industries, as you can imagine, because work tends to stop in the rainy season.**

Thank you. What are the main industries?

The main industry is the mass production of cars and buses, which are mostly exported. Plastic items, especially toys, are important exports as well. In fact, we tend to export most of the products that we manufacture.

I see. And what are the main festivals?

Sorry, but can you explain what the word 'festival' means?

It means a special time when communities and families celebrate something.

Thanks. Well, our principal festivals are religious, because most people in my country follow the same religion. We have a three-day festival in summer, when people exchange gifts. We also have

a national Independence Day in January. **On both festivals, families celebrate together and the shops close for several days. So, we need to plan these events carefully, as they take a lot of organising.**

In this second example, the candidate was using more advanced vocabulary (*e.g. humid, tend to, exchange.*) This is one reason why the score would be higher. However, the main reason the Band score is high is because the candidate used a 2-step process to answer the questions.
Let's explain what this means. The candidate said:

It's generally hot and humid, although it rains heavily in October. This has a big influence on our way of life and our industries, as you can imagine, because work tends to stop in the rainy season.

Here the candidate describes the climate and then gives a second, more general piece of information about the climate, telling us about its *influence*. The candidate also used the phrase 'As you can imagine,' which is a typical term used by English speakers to build a rapport during a conversation.

Then the candidate said:

The main industry is the mass production of cars and buses, which are mostly exported. Plastic items, especially toys, are important exports as well. In fact, we tend to export most of the products that we manufacture.

Here, the candidate does something similar: he answers the question and then gives a second, more general piece of information, showing that he has thought about the nature of his country's industries. He does the same thing in the answer to the third question about festivals, with a first piece of information (**our principal festivals are religious . . .**) supported by a further comment (**So we need to plan these events carefully . . .**) showing that he understands the situation.

This is what we call the two-step process for Part 1. This means that you give an initial piece of information, and then a further, more general piece of information showing that you understand the situation or that you have considered the situation.

You'll notice that the answers are roughly three sentences in length. You don't need to give more than three sentences for a Part 1 answer, unless you're very confident that you can speak for a bit longer on the question in structured way. Keeping your answers to roughly three sentences in Part 1 also allows the examiner to ask a wider variety of questions in the time available, which should make it easier for you to answer.

Practising Part 1 Speaking with Example Band 9 Answers

Here are some more examples of Part 1 questions for you to practise. Try to answer the following questions, using the same two-step process. Give an initial answer with one piece of information, and then give another piece of information that shows that you understand the situation you are describing. In the next section of this book, there are two example answers for each of these questions. The first example answer given is a band 5 or 6 answer, and the second one is a band 9 answer.

But try these examples first, before you look at the examples!

Please tell me about your home town. What do people do in the evenings?

Let's talk about your plans for the future. What kind of career do you want to follow?

Tell me about your family. What do they do?

Tell me about your country's food and dishes.

Where are you living at present? What's it like?

What do you like to do at weekends?

Examples of Answering Part 1 Practise Questions

These are not the only possible answers, of course, because each person will have a different reply. The important thing is the two-step structure that the band 9 candidate uses, compared to the band 5 or 6 candidate.

Please tell me about your home town. What do people do in the evenings?

Band 5 or 6: **People go to the main square and drink coffee.**

Band 9: **Many people socialise in the main square, especially in the coffee shops. You could say that the main square is the most important social meeting place, because we don't have a beach or any really big restaurants, as some other towns do.**

Let's talk about your plans for the future. What kind of career do you want to follow?

Band 5 or 6: **I want to be a food scientist, maybe for a big company.**

Band 9: **I plan to be a food scientist if I possibly can, which would mean finishing my degree and joining a large manufacturing company. That's a challenge, but I think my personal skills are well suited to that type of environment.**

Tell me about your family. What do they do?

Band 5 or 6: **My parents are teachers. I have a sister, she is a student.**

Band 9: **My parents are both teachers, and they teach engineering and biology. I think they must have been a big influence on my** sister and myself, because my sister is studying technology and I'm applying to Australian universities to study genetics.

Tell me about your country's food and dishes.

Band 5 or 6: **Our favourite food is meat. Our national dish is a lamb dish, like curry.**

Band 9: **We tend to eat a lot of meat, although these days people are trying to eat less meat for health and environmental reasons. We have a national dish which is similar to lamb curry, but made in a unique way. Not many people know how to make the recipe properly, so eating it is always a special occasion for us.**

Where are you living at present?

Band 5 or 6: **I'm living with two other students in an apartment.**

Band 9: **At the moment I'm renting an apartment with two other students, because we want to be close to the campus, and property in that area is actually quite expensive. I'm pleased with the location, because it's very convenient and it's quiet at night.**

What do you like to do at weekends?

Band 5 or 6: **I play tennis a lot. I go to a club near my house.**

Band 9: **My main activity these days is playing tennis, as I belong to a club near my house. There are a lot of social activities as well as the tennis itself. To be honest, I enjoy the social side as much as the sport, so I really look forward to weekends.**

When reading the above examples, please think about the way that the band 9 candidate answered the questions using the two-step process. She gave a piece of information, and then another piece of information to show that she understands or is thinking about the situation. Note that the answers are generally three sentences. Remember that you don't need an answer in Part 1 that is much longer than about three sentences. The examiner wants to hear you answer as many questions as possible in this part of the test.

Remember too that the questions in Part 1 are always about you and your life. You should have some comments ready to give about any aspect of your life, using the two-step process explained here. Practise with a friend if possible, using the following topics. All of these topics are taken directly from the list of IELTS examiners questions for Part 1.

Your home country – its industries, food and dishes, festivals, climate, geography, education system, media, history, infrastructure and transport arrangements.
(For example, *'Let's talk about transport in your country. How do people generally travel around?'*)

Your home town, city or village – its appearance, population, main businesses, education facilities, public amenities, entertainment possibilities, history.
(For example, *'Regarding your home town, what are the main schools?'*)

Your plans for the future – your planned examinations, work and career, place to live, places you plan to visit, experiences you would like to have.
(For example, *'I'm interested in your future plans. Which job would you like to do? Are there any special exams you will need to pass?'*)

Your family and friends – the jobs that your relatives and friends do, what you like to do when you are with your family or friends, how you keep in touch with your family or friends, your best friend's situation.
(For example, *'Let's discuss your friends. What do you generally do together when you meet them?'*)

Your personal interests – your taste in music, sport, entertainment, art, ways to relax and exercise, food and cooking.
(For example, *'Let's talk about sport. What sports or games are you interested in? Which sports do you play?'*)

Concluding Part 1 Of the Test

At the end of Part 1 (after about three to four minutes) the examiner will say *'That's the end of Part 1. Now we're moving on to Part 2 of the test'* or something similar. You should smile and wait for the instructions for Part 2. Don't worry if you think you made some mistakes in Part 1. Stay positive and try to relax; the examiner will help you feel at ease.

Now we'll move on to strategies for Part 2 of your test.

***

Strategies For Part 2 Of the Speaking Test

In Part 2 (which lasts roughly three to four minutes) the examiner will give you a card which has a topic task for you to talk about. The topic will be about something in your life, past or present. There will also be some brief task instructions on the card. You will have one minute to think about the topic and make some brief notes. The examiner will give you a pencil and paper to make these notes. After your one-minute preparation, the examiner will ask you to speak for between one and two minutes on the topic. When you finish, the examiner will ask some short questions about what you have said.

Here are two different examples of a Part 2 topic task card:

Describe a holiday or trip that you remember well
Say when and where this was
What you did
Who you went there with
And say why you remember this holiday or trip so well.

*

Describe a time when you entered a race or competition
Say when and where this was
What the race or competition involved
What happened at the end of it
And say how you felt about this at the time

The above examples are about something in your past life. It's also possible that the topic will be about something in your present life now. Here are two examples about your present life:

Describe a building or a place you like to visit regularly.
Say what this building or place is like

Where it is
What you do when you go there
And say why you visit it regularly

*

Describe a friend that you are in contact with often
Say who this person is
How you came to know them
How you make contact with him/her
And say why you are often in contact with this person

In the test, check that you understand whether the task instructions are about past or present situations. You may lose marks if you confuse the past and present.

Note that these Part 2 topic tasks are always simple subjects about your life past or present. The topics will never ask about such subjects as your politics, religion or sensitive aspects of your life such as family problems. If for some reason you find the topic embarrassing, you can say so and ask for another topic, saying for example *'I'm sorry, I find it difficult to talk about my school days. Could I please have a different topic?'* The examiner will cooperate with you if this seems necessary. The examiner's objective is always to put you at ease, and to give you every opportunity to speak as naturally as possible.

How To Answer the Part 2 Topic Task

You should use your one minute to prepare notes on what to say. You will see that the topic card always contains a general heading and then four points for you to talk about, for example, *when, where, who and why* or *when, what, how and how you felt.*

In your one-minute preparation, you should make brief notes about the general heading and about each of these four points. Use the paper and pencil that the examiner gives you. Don't worry about writing neatly, because this paper is destroyed at the end of the test. You don't need to write complete sentences, just write a few words to help you remember what to say on each point. Write in English, not your mother language, because this will help to organise your ideas in English.

Here's an example. For the first topic we saw above, here is the topic task card again:

Describe a holiday or trip that you remember well *(general heading)*
Say when and where this was *(point 1)*
What you did *(point 2)*
Who you went there with *(point 3)*
And say why you remember this holiday or trip so well *(point 4)*

Now, here are some notes made on the paper by a successful band 9 candidate during the one-minute preparation time:

Describe a holiday or trip that you remember well *My trip to Paris*

Say when and where this was *2015, summer, school holidays, end of my primary school years*

What you did *We saw Paris, the Eiffel Tower, lots of cafes and museums, river boats*

Who you went there with *School friends and 2 teachers, best friend spoke French*

And say why you remember this holiday or trip so well *End of primary, lots of fun, also sad, very hot, teacher broke his arm*

This example is probably the maximum amount that you can make in the one-minute preparation – but it's enough! The reason for making these notes is to prepare your mind for the Part 2 speaking, to make sure that you cover each of the four points in the topic task, and as a result to show the examiner that you can organise ideas.

How To Use These Notes While Speaking in Part 2

In Part 2, the task instructions tell you to speak for between one and two minutes. You should try to speak for about two minutes. This gives you the maximum chance to demonstrate your speaking ability to the examiner. In reality, if you aim to speak for two minutes, you will probably speak for slightly less time. But if you only aim to speak for one minute, you may speak for less than that, and so you would be below the minimum speaking time.

When you start speaking, you should begin by saying *'I'm going to talk about . . .'* or similar, and then paraphrase the notes you made about the general topic heading. You should speak for roughly thirty seconds on each of the four points you have made notes about in your preparation. The strategy is that four points x roughly thirty seconds each = roughly two minutes of speaking, which is the maximum required. Use this strategy to make sure your speaking is roughly balanced across the four points, and so that you reach the two minutes. It doesn't matter if you speak for a bit less or more than thirty seconds on each of the individual points. Try to make each point as natural as possible.

While speaking, you should maintain friendly eye contact with the examiner, and glance *occasionally* at your notes to make sure that you are covering all the ideas that you noted. You should also glance *occasionally* at your watch to make sure that you are speaking for 30 seconds on each of the four points. Remember, the majority of your eye contact should be with the examiner. If you wish, you can *occasionally* mark the notes on the paper, for example by ticking them with the pencil, as you talk about them. Provided that you keep speaking naturally, and maintain reasonable eye contact, the examiner will not mind this. Please note that we emphasise the word *occasionally!* You shouldn't *constantly* look at your watch or mark the notes, because you are supposed to be speaking *to* the examiner.

You will need a lot of practice to be able to talk naturally for two minutes on these topic tasks, using notes and a watch. Even for a native speaker of English, this can be quite a difficult thing to do.

Band 9 Example of Part 2 Speaking

Here is the transcript of a band 9 candidate speaking for two minutes about the 'holiday or trip' topic task shown above in the previous section. Note how the candidate introduces the general topic, and then speaks about each of the four points in the topic task instructions, using the ideas in his preparation notes to guide the answer.

We have added the relevant parts of the topic task **in bold** so that you can see the structure of the answer. When speaking, you should not read directly from the topic card, but you can paraphrase some of the task instructions, as this candidate does for point 3.

(Describe a holiday or trip that you remember well) 'I'm going to talk about a trip that I remember very well, which was a holiday in Paris, the capital of France.' **(Say when and where this was)** 'This happened in 2015, in August, so it was right in the middle of the school holidays. In fact, at that time I was eleven years old, and I had just finished my primary school education, so the trip was actually organised by my primary school as a way of marking the end of our studies and the fact that we were going on to secondary school, and it was a way of saying goodbye to the teachers as well.

So it was certainly an important and very memorable trip, for lots of reasons.'

(What you did) 'We knew that Paris was a famous city, and of course we quickly saw all the most important tourist sights, such as the Eiffel Tower, which was very impressive and gave us an amazing panoramic view from the platform at the top. We also went on trips on the river boats, which gave us a long tour of the city along the banks of the river, and let us see the people of Paris doing their daily jobs such as running shops and cafes. But we also spent a lot of time in many of the museums, especially the art museums, and we went to a huge range of cafes and restaurants in the evenings. Personally, I found those evenings just as interesting as the big tourist attractions, because we could relax and listen to people speaking French, and we could practice ordering snacks and refreshments in French. This was tricky at first, because we were only eleven and our French was very basic, apart from one person I'll tell you about in a moment. But we soon became more confident.'

(Who you went there with) 'So, who did I travel there with? Well, I went with a group of classmates, in particular my best friend at the time, who spoke French much better than the rest of us, and so he was a big help in getting around. In fact, he enjoyed showing off and impressing people with his French, which surprised the local people, because not many visitors speak the language so well, especially children. We also had two of our primary school teachers, who escorted us around and arranged the excursions and meals and so on. The teachers were kept very busy, as I'm sure you can imagine, but they always stayed positive, and they told us a great deal about the city and its history, which we enjoyed hearing about.'

(And say why you remember this holiday or trip so well) 'The reason I remember this trip so vividly is partly because it was very enjoyable, and it was my first experience of staying in another country for more than a few hours. I remember being nervous at first, and then starting to enjoy all the new things we saw. At the same time, unfortunately, we all felt a bit sad because we knew that our primary school years were finished and we all expected that secondary school would be harder and more demanding for us. I also remember that the weather was extremely hot and humid, especially on the subway and inside the buildings during the day, because nobody in Paris seemed to have air conditioning! I remember thinking that it was really strange for such a modern country not to have proper air-cooling systems. I never found out why that was.

One other reason why I remember this holiday was because one of my teachers had an accident. He was walking down the steps outside a museum when it was raining in a thunderstorm, and he slipped over on the wet stone and broke his arm. He had to go to hospital and have emergency treatment, and I remember thinking he was very brave after that to continue escorting us pupils around with a broken arm in such hot weather. I don't think I would have been so brave and so patient!'

(This candidate spoke for approximately 1 minute 45 seconds)

Important Things to Consider About Part 2

Look again at the task card for this 'holiday or trip' example, and see how the candidate is careful to answer the four different parts of the task (**When, what, who, why**) using the preparation notes.

Note that this candidate does not use very formal or technical vocabulary, apart from phrases that any educated English speaker would use (e.g. *'panoramic view, excursions, demanding.'*) Remember that in the speaking test you don't need to use the academic vocabulary which is necessary in IELTS writing part two. It is more important that the speaking Part 2 answer is clearly structured, the descriptions are relevant to the task and clear, and the content of the answer is understandable.

If you can't remember enough about an aspect of your life for this task, you can invent some details. For example, it's possible that our candidate invented the description of the teacher breaking his arm. If you invent details, you must make them credible and relevant. Don't invent things which are comical or tragic, because this would be too obvious. For example, 'my teacher broke his arm' is credible. 'My teacher was kidnapped by the mafia' is not really credible, and the examiner would disapprove.

Another point is that your Part 2 answer must avoid padding. 'Padding' means saying unnecessary things or giving long lists just to make your answer longer. For example, if the candidate gave a long list of the French places he saw (e.g. *I remember that we saw the Eiffel Tower, the Louvre, the Seine, the Moulin Rouge, Orly airport, the Champs Elysee and the Montmartre district*) or if he gave a list of all the names and ages of his friends, this would be seen as padding. The examiner will immediately start to reduce your mark if you seem to be padding your answer.

Now here's another example of another candidate speaking at band 9 level, answering the example topic card we saw about a building. Note that this task is asking about the present, not the past:

Describe a building or a place you like to visit regularly
(general heading)
Say what this building or place is like (point 1)
Where it is (point 2)
What you do when you go there (point 3)
And say why you visit it regularly (point 4)

The candidate's notes during the one minute preparation time were:

Describe a building or a place you like to visit regularly The sports centre

Say what this building or place is like It's modern and recently built, lots of facilities

Where it is Suburbs, very convenient for the bus, nice area

What you do when you go there Use the gym, table tennis, shower, not the sauna

And say why you visit it regularly Pay my monthly subscription, and I need to keep fit

Now this is the transcript of the candidate speaking:

(Describe a building or a place you like to visit regularly) 'I'd like to talk about the sports centre which I use very often these days.' (**Say what this building or place is like**) 'This is a brand-new sports centre, built just in the last couple of years in fact, and the building is very modern with full air conditioning and a wide range of facilities including a gym, many indoor sports, a swimming pool, a sauna and showers. The lobby is like the entrance to an expensive hotel, it's really very impressive indeed. There's also a restaurant and a park outside for relaxing in, which has a skateboard area too. The staff are very professional and very helpful, and there's a really positive atmosphere to the whole place, which I enjoy.'
(Where it is) 'It's located in one of the suburbs of the town, about a kilometre from the town centre. This is a very pleasant area, which is very safe and generally fairly quiet, so nobody has any worries about going there on their own, especially in the evenings. The sports centre is actually on one of the main bus routes, so it only takes a few minutes to get there from my apartment. There's also a train station nearby, so people come from other towns to use the centre. That means you end up meeting a wide variety of people, not just the same familiar faces all the time.'
(What you do when you go there) 'When I go there, the main thing I do is use the gym. It's very well equipped with exercise machines and weight training equipment, and I tend to go two or three times

a week to do weight training. This means I lift weights and use machines which build up strength in different parts of the body, such as the legs and back, to improve overall fitness as well as physical strength. I also use the table tennis room quite a lot, because I have some friends who are really good at that sport and they're trying to train me up to be at their kind of level. So, on a typical visit I'll do an hour or two in the gym, and then maybe an hour of table tennis if my friends are there. Even if my friends aren't around, there's usually someone who wants to play a quick game or two against me. One thing I always do is use the shower afterwards, because it's an excellent high-pressure shower, which is far better than the one in my apartment. By the time I leave, I'm like a new person, you might say. I've never used the sauna though, because for some reason it just doesn't really appeal to me. Maybe I'll try it out at some point.'

(And say why you visit it regularly) 'One reason I visit the sports centre so regularly is partly because I pay a monthly membership subscription which is quite expensive, so I feel I should get as much use out of it as possible in return for the fee. Sometimes, if I don't feel like going, I tell myself that I'm wasting the subscription money by not being there, and that motivates me. But the main reason is that I really enjoy keeping fit these days, especially as I'm studying full time, so I'm sitting at a desk for most of the day. Without going to the sports centre, especially for the weight training, I'm sure I'd start to have back problems like those people who work in offices and don't take enough exercise. This way, I feel fit even while I'm still at my desk. That's important for my physical health, but it also puts me in a positive and optimistic frame of mind. I feel that's essential for my overall wellbeing.'

(This candidate spoke for approximately 1 minute 35 seconds.)

Practising Part 2 Speaking

Now try these topic tasks as a practice. For each task, work with a friend or another student. Spend one minute making notes on the four points in the topic, and then try to speak for about thirty seconds on each point, referring to your notes to help you remember your ideas, so that your total answer is roughly two minutes. Start by saying *'I'm going to talk about . . .'* Remember to maintain eye contact with your friend and to check your watch and notes *occasionally* to see how the time is progressing.

Describe a meal or gathering that you attended.
Say when this was
Who was present
Why the meal or gathering was organised
And say what you did while you were there

*

Describe a journey that you make regularly
Say where you go
How you travel
Why you make this journey
And say what you do when you arrive at your destination

*

Describe a natural place you have visited or seen
Say where this is
What the place is like
When you visited or saw it
And say why you remember this place

*

Describe an event you remember from your time at school
Say how old you were
What happened
Who was involved
And say why you still remember this event

One final piece of advice about Part 2 is that, if your task card is about an event from the past, you may wish to tell a dramatic story (*dramatic* = surprising and exciting, like a theatre play or movie.) For example, the transcripts in this book for practice tests 4 (about New York) and 14 (about a job interview) tell a story with exciting drama, almost like a little movie script. On the other hand, tests 1 (about a driving test) and 20 (about a train journey) don't tell a dramatic story, they just describe a normal situation. Some people find it easier to speak for two minutes if they have a dramatic story to tell, while other candidates prefer to describe a series of events with nothing unusual. When you do these practice tests, try both options and see which approach you prefer. The examiner will not care which approach you take, as long as you structure your two minutes and answer the task fully in the way we've explained.

After Your Two Minute Speaking in Part 2

In the test, if you speak for two minutes, the examiner will ask you to stop speaking at the two-minute point. The examiner will not let you speak for much more than two minutes, because the test must be time limited. If for some reason you speak for less than one minute, the examiner will ask you to speak for longer, so that you follow the instructions in the topic task.

After this, the examiner will ask a series of simple questions about what you have said. (For example, *'Thank you. Would you recommend Paris as a destination?'* or *'Thank you. What do you remember about the art museums?'*) You should give a brief two-step answer, similar to the answers you gave in Part 1. For example, about the Paris trip:

Thank you. Would you recommend Paris as a destination?

Yes, I would definitely recommend it. It's a very busy city, and it's really quite expensive, but there's certainly a lot to see for people

of all interests and all ages, even though there's no air conditioning, as I mentioned.

Thank you. What do you remember about the art museums?

Well, I remember one museum had the famous painting of the Mona Lisa. It was so popular that it was difficult to see the picture because of all the dozens of other tourists crowding into the room, which was a shame because I really wanted to see it. I think they should have a ticket system to reduce the crowding.

Another example, about the sports centre:

Thanks. Do you do any other sports as well?

Well, I like running, which I do several times a week. I go jogging on the streets near my home, not at an athletics track. I'm not one of those people who's always timing their running and trying to improve, though. I just do it for general fitness and relaxation.

I see. What sort of interests do you have, apart from fitness?

I build gaming computers as a hobby, which is fascinating. That means I order the components online and then assemble them myself, and sometimes I sell the finished computers on to other people for a profit, so you might say it's also a sort of business for me.

When this process is finished, the examiner will say *'That completes Part 2 of the test. Now we'll move on to Part 3'* or something similar, and then take back the task card. You should smile and wait for the next question to begin Part 3.

Strategies For Part 3 Of the Speaking Test

Part 3 (which lasts for roughly four minutes) is a discussion between you and the examiner. The topic will be related to the topic you just spoke about in Part 2, but the questions will be about society in general, *not* about your own life in particular. For example, if the topic in Part 2 was your memory of a holiday or trip, the topic in Part 3 may be about people's holidays or about travel in general. Here are some more examples of Part 2 *personal* topics and the possible Part 3 *general* discussion topics related to them:

<u>Part 2 *personal* topics</u>

Your best friend
A time when you worked in a team
Your plans for a future career
Something you bought
A journey you make often

<u>Possible Part 3 *general* discussion topics</u>

Communicating with friends
Teamwork at work and school
Careers and workplaces
Retail and shopping
Developments in transport

You see from these examples that the Part 3 topics are about people and society in general, *not* about you and your situation personally.

The Different Types of Question in Part 3

When Part 3 begins, the examiner will introduce the topic by saying, for example, *'Now we're going to discuss education and work'* or something similar. The examiner will then ask you a series of questions connected to the topic.

Some of these questions will be about your *opinion* of the topic (for example *'Do you think that young people should have detailed career plans?'*)

Other questions will ask you to suggest some *ideas* on the topic (for example, *'How can schools prepare students for work?'*)

It's very important to answer these two different types of question in the appropriate way.

Answering Part 3 'Opinion' Questions

Here are examples of some 'opinion' type part 3 questions, plus band 9 answers, on the topic of 'education and work':

Examiner: *Do you think that young people should have detailed career plans?*

Candidate: **In some ways, yes, this is important. For example, pupils should think about careers when they choose their exam courses, in addition to what interests them. I think a lot of successful people start thinking about their careers at an early stage these days. But on the other hand, it's difficult to have very precise plans at a young age, because people and opportunities change so rapidly. Overall, I would say that general intentions are useful, but highly detailed career plans are not really relevant.**

Do you think that teachers should use the Internet as part of school lessons?

Well, I think that this can be useful, for example to show the pupils videos or media reports on subjects they are studying. This helps bring a subject to life, and it's very common of course. On

the other hand, though, I wouldn't want a teacher to be constantly searching online or referring to Internet materials all the time during lessons, because it would be distracting or confusing. So, I think that well-chosen Internet resources can be a benefit if used carefully. It's down to the teacher to plan it properly.

Is it useful to have a gap year between school and university?

I think a gap year could be useful for some people, for example to help them learn about work or to get experience of other cultures. What's more, if a student does charity work during a gap year, that's a very positive thing for the person and for society. But there are also examples of young people wasting time on gap years, or even having accidents or getting involved in crime. We see stories about that in the media now and then, some of them quite sad. In general, I think these years can only be useful if they're planned and carried out properly.

Think about how the candidate structures the answers to these 'opinion' type questions. The candidate answers by firstly considering some different sides of the question, and then giving a personal view at the end. This is the best way to answer an 'opinion' type question in Part 3. Remember to consider some different aspects of the question, and then give a logical opinion at the end. Don't be emotional or dramatic, and don't make jokes about the topic.

Please note that these answers are much longer than the Part 1 answers. Part 3 answers are ideally from five to approximately ten sentences long, depending on whether you know a lot about the topic, or if you can think of a lot of points to discuss.

Please note also that there is no 'right' or 'wrong' answer in these Part 3 questions. The examiner will not mark you on your opinion itself, but on the way you present your opinion in a balanced, effective way. For example, it doesn't matter if you think that gap years are a good thing or a bad thing. What matters is that you discuss the different aspects and then reach a reasonable conclusion.

Answering Part 3 'Ideas' Questions

Remember that we said there is another type of question in Part 3, which is an 'ideas' type question. In these questions, the examiner is not asking your opinion, but is asking you to suggest some ideas, which will usually be usually the reasons for a situation, the solutions to a problem or some ways of achieving something.

Here are examples of some 'ideas' type Part 3 questions plus band 9 answers, on the same topic of 'education and work':

Examiner: *How can schools prepare students for work?*

Candidate: **There are several ways that schools can do this. To start with, they can include examples of work and careers in their lessons, so for instance if the subject is chemistry they could study the career of a successful chemist, for example. Schools could also send pupils on visits to workplaces, such as offices or factories, so that the young people can see workers actually doing their jobs. Another thing they could do, for older pupils, is to organise work experience so that students actually try doing a real job for a few hours or days. I think that all these things together would certainly help to prepare young people for work.**

What can teachers use the Internet for in lessons?

I can think of two main uses for the Internet in classrooms. One is to show examples of videos or audio material which let students see a subject in real life. For example, if a class is studying volcanoes, the teacher could show different types of volcanoes around the world, which would be interesting. Another way would

be to let pupils search for information themselves, for example to research the effect of volcanoes on human populations in history, and then report back to the class. Of course, this would have to be managed and monitored pretty closely by the teacher.

Unemployment among young people is a major problem in many countries. Can you suggest any solutions?

Well, I suppose the main solution would be to improve education standards among the young people, by spending more on schools and universities. This would eventually help people find jobs, and hopefully the jobs would be better paid as well. Another step would be to encourage employers to hire more young people, by subsidising their salaries or offering tax breaks to make employing them more affordable. I also think that some countries could reduce unemployment benefits to young people, to stop them living on welfare instead of working. These things are difficult to do, and they might be rather unpopular, but I feel they would work.

Why do some young people want to become teachers?

I imagine the biggest reason is having an interest in helping children to develop, by teaching them useful knowledge and skills. There's probably also a desire to share an interest in a specific subject, and to expand the knowledge of this subject in society generally. For example, music teachers are very enthusiastic about music and they want more people to appreciate it. And finally, I think that, for some young people, there's also a third reason, which is an urge to be a positive role model for youngsters. So, there's a range of possible motivations.

Note that in these examples, the candidate is *not* giving a personal *opinion* (e.g. saying if something is good or bad, useful or not useful) because the question doesn't ask for that. The candidate is quickly thinking of two or three *ideas* on the topic, and explaining them in a logical way. This is the best way to answer 'ideas' questions in Part 3. Listen carefully to the question, think of two or three relevant ideas, and explain why they are relevant to the question. If you can think of some examples to support the ideas (e.g. the example of 'music teachers' above) that's good, but remember not to give personal stories or personal information in Part 3. Remember: Part 1 and Part 2 are about you *personally*; but Part 3 is about your opinions and ideas on society *generally*.

As with the 'opinion' type of Part 3 questions, there is no 'right' or 'wrong' answer. For example, the examiner isn't expecting you to have a certain suggestion about why people become teachers, and it doesn't matter if the examiner agrees with you personally or not. The important thing is the quality of the answer you give.

You must be ready to answer a combination of 'opinion' and 'ideas' questions in Part 3, because the examiner will probably ask you both types of question. For example, the examiner may ask an 'opinion' question and then an 'ideas' question and so on, in any sequence.

Please note that the examiner will also react to things you say, for example by saying *'That's interesting, can you tell me more?'* or *'I see, but what about the negative aspect?'* or similar things. This is because Part 3 is intended to be a realistic discussion, where one comment leads to further comments. The examiner will respond flexibly to your remarks, in order to encourage you to speak more. They won't just read the questions from their list, because that would be artificial.

However, don't try to ask the examiner for their views or ideas. Don't say *'What do you think?'* or *'Can you think of anything else?'* The examiner will not respond to this, and you will be losing valuable time.

Practising the Part 3 Questions

Here are some more examples of Part 3 questions, on the topic of 'stores and shopping.' For each question, try to decide quickly if the question is an 'opinion' or an 'ideas' question, and then give an answer in at least five sentences, as you saw in the examples above. In the next section of this book, there are examples of band 9 answers to these questions. As always, these examples are not the only possible answers!

Which are better, small local stores or big supermarkets?

How do stores persuade people to spend money?

Should we allow advertising aimed at children?

Why do people like shopping during sale or promotion times?

What are the advantages of shopping on line? Are there any possible disadvantages or risks?

Should all shops have facilities for disabled people?

Continue to the next section for the example answers.

Part 3 Questions with Band 9 Example Answers

Which are better, small local shops or big supermarkets? (Opinion question)

I think it depends on a person's individual needs. For example, for elderly people, or if someone doesn't have a car, local shops are probably more convenient, and the personal service might also be better in terms of advice and assistance. On the other hand, though, large supermarkets are cheaper and offer a much bigger range of products to choose from. It's also more convenient to buy everything you need in one place. Overall, I think that for most people the supermarkets are probably the best option, because of the affordability and choice they offer.

How do stores persuade people to spend money? (Ideas question)

I think they use a variety of methods. They often use promotions which make people buy more, for example 'Three for the price of two' and so on. These offers are usually backed up with advertising, whether on TV, the Internet or in the shop itself, and the advertising emphasises the money the shopper can save. There is another method too, which is to display the products in an attractive way that encourages shoppers to pick them up and look at them. When they're used together, I think these techniques can be very powerful indeed, and very effective at persuading the public to spend more.

Should we allow TV advertising aimed at children? (Opinion question)

Well, on the one hand, companies should be free to communicate with their customers, and that includes children. We also sometimes forget that children love TV commercials for all the excitement and humour they provide. But on the other hand, children don't have the ability to judge or choose in the way that adults do. Adverts can exploit this weakness, especially if they get the children to start spending pocket money on things they don't really need. So, generally speaking, I think we should allow these adverts, provided they're carefully regulated and controlled by the authorities.

Why do people like shopping during sale or promotion periods? (Ideas question)

I think we're all familiar with the fun of finding a bargain and feeling we've saved money. This is probably the main reason. To be frank, I think another reason is the feeling of following the crowd. I mean, if we see thousands of other people heading to the shops, or commenting about Black Friday deals, we have an urge to do the same thing, even if we don't really need to buy a product. I think that's called 'herd instinct.' Yes, I think those are the two major reasons.

What are the advantages of online shopping over shopping in stores? (Ideas question)

I can think of several advantages of shopping by Internet. For one thing, it tends to be cheaper than in-store, and that's a huge attraction. Besides that, using the Internet is much quicker and more convenient, because we don't have to travel or spend time in town centres, so it's better for the environment too in some respects. The third advantage is the ability to compare products very quickly for quality and price, and so make the best choice possible in the time available. These are the main advantages, I think.

Are there any possible disadvantages or risks? (Ideas question)

Well, the biggest danger is the risk of fraud, because criminals might access your payment details or other personal data when you buy online. The other problem is that you don't actually see the product until it's delivered, so you might find it's different from what you expect in terms of the colour, the texture and so on. That's quite a common problem, in fact, especially for clothing. When that happens, we have the inconvenience and cost of returning the items again. So people need to approach online shopping a bit carefully, to avoid risks and disappointment.

Should all shops have facilities for disabled people? (Opinion question)

There are two sides to this. I agree with people who say that disabled access should be available wherever possible, so that disabled people can go shopping just like everyone else. That's only fair, of course. But on the other hand, some shops are in locations where it would be impossible or incredibly expensive to install things like lifts and ramps, for example in historic buildings or in remote sites. I think we need to make an exception for places like that, but all other shops should certainly have these facilities.

Concluding and Reviewing the IELTS Speaking Test

At the end of Part 3, the examiner will say *'Thank you for your answers. We've now reached the end of the speaking test'* or something similar, and then show you to the exit door. You should smile, say *'Thank you for your time'* and offer to shake the examiner's hand if that's appropriate for you.

After you leave the exam room, it is a good idea to relax and spend some time thinking about your performance in the test. This is because the techniques you use in the speaking test are similar to techniques you should use in real-life situations such as seminars, professional discussions and meetings in English-speaking situations. Of course, it's also possible that you might need to take the IELTS test again until you achieve the band you need. Reviewing the test like this will also help you improve your performance next time. Ask yourself:

Did I engage with the examiner and build a rapport as soon as we met?

Did I present myself in a professional way? Did I speak calmly and maintain reasonable eye contact?

Did I listen carefully to questions and identify the main points?

Did I answer all parts of the questions?

In Part 1, did I show that I understand the situations I described, using the two-step process?

In Part 2, did I organise my description using my notes? Did I then use the notes to help my speaking? Was my description structured around the points on the task card?

In Part 3, did I show that I understand the difference between 'opinion' questions and 'ideas' questions? Did I consider the different aspects of 'opinion' topics, and did I give two or three logical ideas for 'ideas' topics?

Did I use the most advanced English possible for me? Did I ask for clarification in an appropriate way?

Did I learn any new vocabulary, or did I notice that I need some vocabulary on a certain topic?

Now it's time to start using our twenty practice tests to apply the methods we've explained so far.

***

Twenty Complete Practice Tests and Band 9 Example Answers

At this point, we've explained the full range of our strategies for you to use in the speaking test. These methods have been used successfully by IELTS candidates all over the world to achieve the score they need in IELTS speaking. The next section in this book contains twenty complete speaking tests for you to practice and improve your score. After each test, there's a transcript (= a written copy) of a band 9 candidate taking the entire test, so that you can compare your performance to a band 9 example.

How to Use These Tests to Improve Your Band Score

Use these tests with a friend or another student of English. You should both read the sections of this book up to this point, but not beyond this point yet. Decide which one of you will be the examiner, and which one the candidate. Then, get ready to do Practice Test 1. Try to do this test under exam conditions, which means that:

You are in a quiet room with no interruptions
You each have a watch or a clock
You're sitting at a desk or table
There is a pencil available for Part 2 of the test

To get the most from each test, do the test *before* you look at the transcript, not afterwards.

The person being the candidate should not read the questions for Part 1 or Part 3 from the book, because obviously that's not what happens in the test. The person being the examiner should read these questions aloud while the candidate listens and speaks. For Part 2, the 'examiner' should show the candidate the task card, and then allow one minute for making notes and preparation. This book has a separate 'candidate's page' for each test, to make this realistic. The 'examiner' should cut this page from the book and give it to the candidate at the start of Part 2, but not before. The page contains space for making the one-minute notes.

Remember that in each part of the test, the 'examiner' will use the prepared questions (E.g. *'Let's discuss your education. What exams have you taken?'*) but they must also respond flexibly to what the candidate says (E.g. *'That's interesting. Why did you study that?'* etc.) This is how the real test works, by combining the prepared questions with flexibility from the examiner. When you read the band 9 transcripts in this book, you'll see that the examiner often changes or moves away from the prepared questions, to keep the conversation natural and flowing freely.

When you have completed parts 1 to 3 of the practice test, there are two things to do. First, the 'examiner' should give some feedback to the candidate, comparing their performance to the strategies and examples you have both read in this book. For example,

'In Part 1, you sometimes gave two-step answers, which were very effective, but not always. You should do that for all the questions. In Part 2, you spoke for two minutes, which is good, but you didn't cover the second point on the task card, and you went away from the topic at the end. In Part 3, your 'opinion' answers were well organised and thorough, but your 'ideas' answers were too short and only offered one single idea each time.'

Secondly, you should then read through the complete transcript of a band 9 candidate answering the practice test you have just done. While reading, try to see how the candidate uses the strategies we have explained in this book in each part of the test. In particular, look for:

In Part 1, the structure of the two-step answers, the way the examiner tries to make the conversation realistic and how a successful candidate responds.

In Part 2, the connection between the parts of the task and the notes the candidate makes. This will lead on to the structure of the candidate's Part 2 answer, with each part of the task being covered fully.

In Part 3, the way the candidate answers 'opinion' and 'ideas' questions differently, to make sure their answer is as full as possible. You'll see that the candidate discusses both sides of an 'opinion' question, and usually makes three points for an 'ideas' question.

In each practice test, there will also be a lot of vocabulary on some of the very common topics in IELTS, such as education, health, leisure, the environment and careers. For example, practice test 2 has vocabulary on leisure, vacations and travel, and practice test 4 has vocabulary on health and diets. If you meet new vocabulary on these important topics, check the meaning with a dictionary and note the words to use in future.

After you read each transcript, it's a good idea to pause for a while and summarise in your own mind the changes you can take to improve your performance in the next practice test. Don't rush through the tests, but use each one to make every possible improvement to the way you respond to the questions and tasks. In this way, each of these twenty tests will take you a step closer to achieving the band score you need.

***

Practice Test 1

Part One

Let's talk about spare time activities. What do you do in your free time?
What do your friends like doing?
What's your favourite kind of food?
What would you like to do in the future?
Would you need further qualifications to do that?

Part 2

Task card

Describe a time when you gave someone a gift.
Say who this person was
Why you wanted to give them a gift
What gift you decided to give
And say what their reaction was

Examiner's follow up questions

What is this person doing now?
Have you given anyone else a similar gift?

Part 3

Let's discuss giving gifts. Do you think school children should give gifts to their teachers?
How could employers use gifts to motivate and reward their workers?
Do you think giving gifts is an important part of family life?
How do stores and manufacturers use the idea of free items to attract customers?

***

Practice Test 1: Candidate's Page ✂

The examiner should cut this page from the book and give it to the candidate in Part 2, but not before

Part 2 Task card

Describe a time when you gave someone a gift.
Say who this person was
Why you wanted to give them a gift
What gift you decided to give
And say what their reaction was

Space for Candidate to Make Notes in One-Minute Preparation Time

Band 9 Example of Practice Test 1

Part One

Examiner: Hello, good afternoon.

Candidate: Good afternoon, it's nice to meet you.

Can I check your ID, please?

Yes, of course. This is my passport.

Thank you. Now, for Part 1 of our test, let's talk about spare time activities. What do you do in your free time?

If I get the chance, I do enjoy yoga sessions. I find yoga helps me stay very flexible and keeps my posture strong, which is important because my work is desk-based. I also like aerobic exercise, which I do at a local health club at weekends.

Thanks. What about your friends, what do they like doing?

We eat out together quite a lot. There's a big group of us who've been friends since high school, and we like trying different types of cuisine, going to new places and tasting new kinds of dishes. This always gives us something to talk about, on top of catching up on everyone's news and gossip.

And what's your favourite kind of food?

Do you mean what nationality?

Either the nationality or just the type of food.

Well, I like food that's fairly hot and spicy, so I'm a big fan of Mexican and Indian cuisine. I like the way Mexican dishes involve wraps and tacos with different fillings, and I enjoy trying all the different Indian curries with rice. I wouldn't be able to prepare any of those at home, though, because my kitchen is really quite basic at the moment.

So, what food do you cook for yourself?

Oh, it's very bland, to be honest. I can cook straightforward chicken and vegetable meals, which my mother showed me how to do. But a lot of the time I live on sandwiches and omelettes, or stuff from the microwave. You can probably see why I like eating out with my friends.

Yes. You mentioned your kitchen, where are you living at the moment?

I'm sharing an apartment in the city centre with two friends from work. It's basic, as I said, but at least it's clean and it's certainly very secure. It's only a few streets away from the lab where we work, so it's incredibly convenient. I certainly wouldn't want to move accommodation, at least for the time being.

You work in a lab? What does that involve?

I'm an optical technician, which means we analyse the quality of different types of optical equipment such as glasses, binoculars and microscopes. It's a very interesting job, as you can imagine, and the company running the lab seems to have lots of opportunities for the future.

And what would you like to do in the future?

Well, I'm considering relocating to Britain and working in the optical lens industry there. That would be a big change, of course, and the paperwork's extremely complicated these days. I think, on the career side, it would be a real step forward, although from a personal point of view it's a bit daunting. I'm actually still thinking about the whole question of what to do next.

Thanks. Would you need further qualifications to do that?

I'd need to meet the IELTS requirement, but other than that my existing qualifications would be recognised, and they'd be enough to get me through the visa process. That's a big positive for me, because I definitely wouldn't want to go back to college to take more qualifications. Frankly, I'd rather stay working here than have to do that.

Do you know anyone in Britain?

Yes, I have a family friend who lives there and is now a naturalised citizen. She lives near London, so, if I do move over there, I'll probably stay with her at first, because that's where most of the UK optical industry is centred.

Thank you. That's the end of Part 1. Now, in Part 2, I'm going to give you a card with a topic for you to speak about for between one and two minutes. You have a minute to prepare, and you can make notes if you wish.

Part 2

Task card:

Describe a time when you gave someone a gift.
Say who this person was
Why you wanted to give them a gift
What gift you decided to give
And say what their reaction was

Candidate's notes during one minute preparation

My cousin, 3 years ago, driving test 3rd attempt
Because she helped me pass test - lessons, advice, using her car
New computer monitor, gaming, old one not working properly
Pleased, delighted, new games (family reaction though)

Examiner: Well, can you please start speaking on the topic now, for between one and two minutes.

Candidate: Yes, I'm going to talk about a present I bought for my cousin. She's a lovely person, a few years older than me, and she's always been a bit of a mentor to me, as well as being a great friend and good company. Well, this took place three years ago when I was trying to pass my driving test. Up to that point, I'd already taken the test twice, and failed both times. I found that enormously frustrating, because most of my friends were passing on the first or second time, so I felt under quite a bit of pressure to get it right on the third attempt. It was made even more difficult because my parents didn't have a car I could practice in, as we live in the city centre. My cousin, by the way, had passed first time and she even had her own car.

Well, anyway, my cousin could see I was getting a bit stressed by the situation, and she took me under her wing, you might say, and helped me get ready for the test. That meant that she picked me up in her car and let me practice driving around, so that I didn't have to pay for more professional driving lessons, which actually get very expensive after two failed attempts. The cost really adds up. With her, I could rehearse all the manoeuvres that the test requires, and she gave me plenty of practice at driving in traffic and over intersections, which I wasn't very confident about. She gave me lots of advice too, about how to watch out for other cars and avoid any problems which might make me fail again. And sure enough, I actually did manage to pass the test. It was a huge relief, and gave me a great sense of achievement as well.

That's why I wanted to get my cousin a present, to say thank you for all the help and support. The gift I decided to give her was a new computer monitor. That was because she spends a lot of time on her desktop PC, studying, working and playing games as well. The monitor she had at the time was quite outdated, and the screen was a long way from being perfect. So I chose a brand new monitor, which was ultra high definition and one of the largest sizes available. It also curved around the user slightly, so you felt you were immersed in whatever was on the screen. It wasn't cheap, of course, but I was so grateful for passing the test that I decided to really splash out on this present for her. I remember I wrapped the box up in shiny paper, and put it on her PC desk for her to open.

As for her reaction, well she was absolutely thrilled with it. She plugged it in straight away and spent ages showing me how wonderful the image was and how sharp and clear everything looked. I have to say the difference with the previous screen was amazing – not just for gaming, but for work as well. Now, to be honest, this led to a little bit of friction with her parents, my uncle and aunt. Because my cousin was so delighted with it, she started spending even more time than usual on her PC, which her parents rather disapproved of. Fortunately, the novelty wore off after a few weeks, and she didn't turn into one of those people who sit at their computer for every spare minute of the day. She commented to me later on that it had really made a difference to her life, and of course getting a driving license had made a huge difference to me, so I felt that the gift was exactly right for that situation.

(The candidate spoke for 1 minute 35 seconds.)

Examiner: Thank you. Do you have a car these days?

Candidate: I don't actually. Living so centrally, I don't really need one, and parking is a continual struggle in the city centre. But I've hired a car on holiday several times, and that's been incredibly useful to be able to do.

That's nice. Whereabouts did you go on holiday?

I went to Germany with my parents to visit some relatives, and we hired a car at the airport and I drove us around for the whole week. So, I felt very important, and it was a lot of fun, because driving in Germany is completely straightforward. Everybody follows the rules all the time, it's remarkable.

Is that different from your country?

Oh, absolutely, yes. At home, cars are always switching lanes and speeding and so on. I think that's one reason I failed the test twice, because the roads are really difficult to drive on and the traffic is so unpredictable.

I see. And are you a fan of computer gaming, like your cousin?

I'm not really that interested in gaming. I find it difficult to concentrate for the length of time needed to get really good at a game, and if you're not an expert I find it's not very enjoyable. On top of that, the price of those games is pretty extortionate these days.

Well, yes. What's your cousin doing now?

She works as a logistics manager for our national airline, which is demanding but very rewarding apparently. She also has a small child, and she's become quite a well-known blogger about family issues. She's built up a huge number of followers, it's very impressive.

Thanks for that. That's the end of Part 2.

Part 3

Now, in Part 3, let's talk about giving gifts. For example, do you think school children should give gifts to their teachers?

Candidate: Well, the question may sound simple, but there are two sides to that. On the one hand, why shouldn't children show their gratitude and appreciation at the end of term to a teacher who's helped and supported them? It's a very natural and sweet thing to do, you might say. But on the other hand, in some cases this has got out of control. We often hear anecdotally about schools where children bring in really expensive gifts for the teachers, obviously provided by the parents in the background. Sometimes it's almost as if the parents are competing with each other to see which family gives the most lavish presents, or even trying to bribe the teachers to give their child better grades. Any suspicion of that can't be allowed, obviously. Overall, I think schools need a policy to restrict the cost of gifts and make them less expensive. For example, and

I'm thinking aloud because I've only just thought of this now, maybe gifts should be permitted, but the gift should only be something that the child has personally made, like a card or a bunch of flowers from the garden. That might keep things less controversial.

Interesting, thanks. What might be the effect on the school if the gifts do get out of control, as you described?

There would be several effects, some potentially quite serious. For one thing, there might be unhealthy rivalry between children to see who could provide the most expensive present. If that happened, then children from poorer families would probably start to feel inadequate, which is the last thing we want to see. There's also the danger that teachers themselves might be affected by all this, and start to treat children differently depending on the gift they received. Teachers are only human, after all. And we shouldn't forget the parents, either, who might start to focus more on thinking up expensive presents than worrying about the quality of their children's education. All in all, it could be really quite destabilising for a school.

I see. What about at work, how could employers use gifts to motivate and reward their workers?

Well, using gifts as prizes and rewards is certainly an established practice. Employers can set incentives, so that staff who achieve certain levels of sales or productivity will receive a prize, which could be cash or something like a holiday. In South America, they even give employees new cars if they hit certain sales targets, I think. But of course, it doesn't have to be all about sales and profit. Companies can also reward staff with gifts if they get excellent feedback from customers about their warmth and quality of customer service. In industries like hotels and catering, that's especially important. So, employers can use gifts to boost target achievement and also customer care.

What about in a family setting, do you think giving gifts is an important part of family life?

I think we'd all instinctively say yes to that question, but at the same time we need to be a little bit careful. Of course, there are events such as birthdays and certain religious festivals when giving gifts is traditional, so we want to maintain those customs. And, of course, everyone loves getting presents on their birthday, no matter what age you are. But another aspect is the way that these events have become very commercialised in recent years. I'm thinking in particular of Christmas in the English-speaking countries, which is a massive commercial event now, and the busiest time of the year for retail stores. I also think that, in many countries, even birthdays have become quite commercialised, where people feel under pressure to give increasingly expensive and luxurious gifts to family members, especially children. So, all in all, I'd say that yes, gifts are an important part of how a family works, but we should be wary of turning this into a shopping expedition, which only benefits retailers.

Thanks. Speaking of shopping, how do stores and manufacturers use the idea of free items to attract customers?

Oh, this is done quite often. For example, retailers offer a free product if a shopper buys several other products. This encourages consumers to stock up on those products while they're in the store, even if they won't need the product itself for a while. Companies also offer free gifts with purchases, which we see quite often on expensive products such as cosmetics, where you're offered a free gift for buying something new which the manufacturer wants to promote. Some of those free gifts can be quite expensive in themselves. One other way that companies do this is to offer free items or services as part of a loyalty scheme, to keep the customer using their service. The biggest example of this is probably 'air miles' or 'frequent flyer points,' which so many people collect. These can be traded in for free flights or holidays eventually, which is a kind of gift from the airline in return for spending all that money on plane tickets. So, there are several ways that gifts are used to attract customers and also keep them loyal.

Do you see any negative aspects to programmes like 'frequent flyer points?'

Potentially, yes. For one thing, it can take years and years to finally collect enough points to get even one free flight. So as a customer you're giving years of loyalty in return for quite a small reward at the end. Another problem is that the rules for these schemes are constantly changing, so, when someone thinks they have enough points for a certain flight, they may actually be a long way short, because the points required have changed. There's another issue too, specific to airlines, which is that these schemes may be encouraging people to take flights unnecessarily, increasing carbon emissions for no real reason. All these aspects are potential problems, which people need to think about before signing up.

I see. Well, thank you, that's the end of Part 3, and we've finished the speaking test now.

Okay, thanks for your time.

***

Practice Test 2

Part 1

Examiner's questions

What leisure activities are popular in your country?
What kind of food is popular in your country?
Is there a special national dish? Can you describe it?
What is the climate like in your home town?
What amenities does your home town have for the public?

Part 2

Task card

Describe a journey that you have made
Say when this was and where you went
How you travelled
What you did and saw on the journey
And say how you felt at the end of it

Examiner's follow-up questions

Would you recommend this as a method of travelling?
Do you think you will make that journey again in future?

Part 3

How has travel changed over recent years?
Is it better to have holidays in our home countries or to go abroad?
Do you think that tourism damages the environment?
What skills and qualities would a good tour guide need?

***

Practice Test 2: Candidate's Page ✂

**The examiner should cut this page from the book and give it
to the candidate in Part 2, but not before**

Part 2 Task card

Describe a journey that you have made
Say when this was and where you went
How you travelled
What you did and saw on the journey
And say how you felt at the end of it

Space for Candidate to Make Notes in One-Minute Preparation Time

Band 9 Example of Practice Test 2

Part 1

In Part 1, let's talk about your home country. What leisure activities are popular there?

Our national sport is football, and it's certainly a national passion, you might say. Almost everyone watches it on TV, and the stadiums are absolutely packed every Saturday, which shows how popular it is.

Are you a big football fan, yourself?

Well, up to a point. I follow the football when it's livestreamed, and I do enjoy watching it in our local bar with lots of other people. But I'm not interested enough to buy a season ticket or travel to matches like some of my friends.

I see. And what other activities do people like in your country?

Water sports are very popular, because the climate is ideal and there are so many of us living on the coast. Apart from that, movies are also a big interest for us, and the cinemas always seem very busy, even during the week.

Is there a cinema in your home town or city?

Oh yes, a very impressive one, which is a building from the 1930s which has been beautifully preserved. Sometimes visitors come to our town just to look at the cinema building, which gives you some idea of how elegant it is.

Thanks. And what's the climate like in your home town?

It's very warm for most of the year, but we also get a pleasant breeze coming from the sea. We're lucky to be located right on the beach, because further inland it gets extremely hot – uncomfortably hot, in fact.

And what are the main business or industries in your town?

Fishing used to be the main industry, but that's declined in recent times because of competition from neighbouring fishing ports which undercut our prices. The main business today is tourism. The hotels are the biggest employers by far, you see.

What kind of amenities does the town have for tourists?

Sorry, what does that mean, amenities?

It means facilities for people to use.

Thanks. Well, the big attraction is the beach and its water sports, such as surfing and jet ski hire. There are several leisure centres too, and tennis coaching is very popular. Oh, and of course the historic cinema, as I mentioned.

Yes. Do you play tennis yourself?

Unfortunately, I'm having physiotherapy at the moment for an ankle injury, which means I can't put pressure on it in sports like tennis. That's a shame, because I played a lot of tennis in high school, and I really enjoyed it.

Sorry to hear that.

Well, I should be able to play again in about six months. I don't want to rush it, though, so I'm being very cautious.

Thanks, that's the end of Part 1. Now, in Part 2, I'm going to give you a card with a topic for you to speak about for between one and two minutes. You have a minute to prepare, and you can make notes if you wish.

Part 2

Task card

Describe a journey that you have made
Say when this was and where you went
How you travelled
What you did and saw on the journey
And say how you felt at the end of it

Candidate's notes during one minute preparation

Journey to wedding 2 years ago, mountains, lodge
Minibus/coach for the family, all the equipment on board, luxury, pleased with it
Different places for stop offs, countryside, farms, animals, mountains
Eating at roadside
Not very tired, excited, coach was comfortable

Okay, can you please speak to me about the topic now, for between one and two minutes.

Well, I'm thinking of a journey I made two years ago when I was seventeen years old, around the time I started high school. It was in the summer, just after our main national holiday, but before school started again in the autumn. And the journey was to a wedding of one of my cousins, a man who's just a few years older than me, and he was getting married to a lady he met at university. Now, my cousin is very popular in our family, because he's a very intelligent and charming kind of person, one of those people that everybody likes and always invites to any kind of gathering because he's good company. Of course, we were all fascinated to meet this woman he was marrying, to see what she was like and whether she was similar to him in that way. The wedding itself was going to be held in a village in the mountains where she was from, about four hundred kilometres from our town. So, it was quite a major journey, as you can tell.

Well, because so many of us in our family and among our friends wanted to go to the wedding, we ended up hiring a private minibus to take us there. I say minibus, but it was more like a coach, with maybe fifty seats on board. Our group was about thirty people, so we had plenty of space to stretch out and move around. The coach itself was very well equipped, in fact it was really quite luxurious. The seats were like business class seats on a plane, and there was an entertainment screen in front of you, and an attendant who would bring you refreshments if you asked. There was a bathroom on board and air conditioning, which was essential because the weather was very humid indeed, as we were going inland. All in all, we were delighted with the standard of the coach, because some of us had been expecting an old bus or something like that.

And it was a good thing the coach was so comfortable, because in total the journey took about eleven hours to get there. We made pretty fast progress out of our town and onto the freeway, but after a while we left the big roads and we had to head across country towards the mountains where the wedding was going to be. This meant going quite slowly on small local roads through villages and fields, but I don't think any of us minded that really. We passed the time talking and imagining what the wedding would be like, and also watching the countryside through the windows. That was very interesting, because we saw how the farming communities inland were organised, with people tending to the different kinds of animals, and harvesting their crops and so on. I spent ages watching all that going on, and seeing what hard work it was for the farmers, especially when they were herding cattle or sheep in the hills. I was so interested in that, I hardly used my entertainment screen at all.

We also stopped off a few times so that people could stretch their legs and buy something to eat at the side of the road. The food that was on offer in the roadside places was simple, but beautifully cooked and full of flavour. You could tell it was all made from local ingredients and cooked to old family recipes, and of course the cooks enjoyed telling us about how these recipes were handed down to them, and how long it took to make the food. We all agreed it was some of the best food we'd ever had, outside of our own homes.

Finally, late in the evening, we got to this place in the mountains and we pulled up at the lodge where we were staying. And how did I feel at that point? Well, I must say I didn't feel especially tired at all. The coach was so relaxing to be in that the journey wasn't physically tiring, and the occasional stops had broken it up very nicely. So, getting off the coach, I felt very relaxed and ready for anything. As you might expect, we were all very excited as well, and looking forward to the wedding the next day very much. The wedding itself was a lovely ceremony, and I felt that the coach journey had been the best possible way of getting there.

(The candidate spoke for approximately 1 minute 30 seconds.)

Thanks. Would you recommend that as a good method of travel?

Yes, definitely. Provided the coach is modern and well-equipped, it's very pleasant indeed. The problems come when it's an older version without all the equipment, and I'm sure that can be quite stressful on a long trip.

Yes. Will you have any reason to make that particular trip again, to the mountains?

Probably not, as it's not really a place people go to without a very specific reason. But I'd like to go inland more often, because living on the coast it's not a way of life we see often. Our country is very sharply divided between the coast and inland lifestyles, you see.

I see. Oh, and what was your cousin's wife like, after all that?

She's just like him, very clever and very charming. Her family are all very nice as well, they made us feel very welcome indeed.

Thanks. That's the end of Part 2, so now we'll go to Part 3 and talk about travel.

Part 3

How has travel changed over recent years?

Let's see. Probably the biggest change has been the adoption of electric vehicles, especially cars and buses. These vehicles can make travelling much cleaner and more efficient, especially in urban situations, although they're still very expensive to buy, and their range outside of cities is pretty limited. Another change has been the increased use of trains between cities and even between countries, as people seem to be flying less. The reasons for that are partly environmental worries, but probably also just the increasingly high cost of flying. And a third change, maybe, is that in general people are actually starting to travel less and less for work, because so much can be done over Zoom that commuting is becoming less essential. In fact, the Covid pandemic played a big part in that development as well.

You mentioned the environment, so in what ways does travel damage the environment?

Oh, in several ways, especially by producing carbon emissions and other pollution which can have serious consequences, both long and short term. That's why carbon offsetting is such a growth area these days, to reduce the overall impact of emissions. But there are other harmful effects too, for example the noise pollution that comes from aircraft in particular. There's also the destruction of natural habitats that happens when land is used to build new roads, rail lines or airports. All of these problems combine to make travel an issue that has to be planned and managed responsibly. That doesn't mean we shouldn't travel or have vacations, but they need to be responsible.

Thanks. And about vacations – do you think it's better to go on holiday abroad or in one's home country?

I think it depends on a person's tastes and needs. If someone wants a complete change of scene, and maybe to try out new languages and new lifestyles, then going abroad is a good way to achieve that. A lot of people would agree that experiencing another culture is very good for you psychologically, even if it's only for one or two weeks. But on the other hand, not everyone wants to be challenged like that on every holiday! Sometimes you just want to relax and take it easy, and maybe catch up with friends and family, or see somewhere new without having to try speaking another language, which can be stressful. So, I'd say either option can be suitable, depending on the individual and the circumstances at the time.

I see, yes. What qualities would someone need to be a good tourist guide?

To be a tourist guide? Well, for a start, you'd need to be a very friendly and approachable person, able to communicate with all kinds of different people. You'd also need to be very flexible, because presumably you'd be working a variety of hours and in many different places. On top of that, tour guides have to be very well organised, because obviously there's a huge risk if an excursion gets lost or if someone gets left behind in a strange place. I suppose one other point is that they have to be quite knowledgeable and well-informed about the place they're showing people around. That's because they're going to get all kinds of questions about the history, the reasons for this and that, and they have to be ready to answer all these questions confidently. They can't say, 'I'll Google it and get back to you, ma'am.' All in all, it's probably quite a demanding job.

Do you think the job of a tour guide has changed much in recent years?

In some ways it must have changed. For example, these days there will tend to be a wider mix of nationalities in tour groups than a few years ago, so the guide will need to have an understanding of more languages. That makes me realise that there might be more tensions inside a multinational tour group, because there's so much conflict and dispute between different countries in the world these days. So, a guide might have to become more of a diplomat as well, in a small-scale way. But in other respects, such as the interpersonal skills and the organisation, the job is probably still much the same compared to, say, twenty years ago.

Thanks. That completes Part 3, and we've finished the speaking test now.

***

Practice Test 3

Part 1

Examiner's questions

What were your favourite subjects at school? Why?
Do you plan to study more in future? What/ why?
Do your friends work or study? What do they do?
How do you keep in touch with your friends and family?
What use do you make of social media?

Part 2

Task card

Describe something you bought which you were not happy with
Say what you bought and from where
Why you were not happy with it
What you did about this
And say what happened as a result

Examiner's follow up questions

Would you buy from the same place or source again?
Have you bought similar products since then?

Part 3

How has the Internet changed the way people shop?
How can people protect themselves when shopping online?
Do supermarkets have too much power these days?
What skills would a person need to run a very large, busy store?

***

Practice Test 3: Candidate's Page ✂

The examiner should cut this page from the book and give it to the candidate in Part 2, but not before

Part 2 Task card

Describe something you bought which you were not happy with
Say what you bought and from where
Why you were not happy with it
What you did about this
And say what happened as a result

Space for Candidate to Make Notes in One-Minute Preparation Time

Band 9 Example of Practice Test 3

Part 1

In this first part, please tell me about yourself. What were your favourite subjects at school?

Oh, I think my best subjects were definitely maths and geography. Of those two, geography was my favourite, and in fact I ended up doing it at university level, which I've just completed.

And why do you enjoy geography so much?

It's fascinating, because it combines things like climate and geology with concepts like economics. At least, it does at degree level. At school, it was much more about volcanoes and glaciers and so on, which are interesting topics in themselves.

I see. And do you plan to study more in future?

I'd like to, but I think it's time to concentrate on starting my career at this point. Studying is great, but there's the financial aspect I have to think about as well.

Of course. What career are you focussed on now?

Well, I work at a water treatment services company. That means we produce filters for water purification systems, which are then sold all over the world to all kinds of different customers and countries.

That sounds interesting.

It's very interesting, yes. I'm only a trainee, but I've already helped to set up a production line for a new kind of filter which is being exported. It's certainly a company I want to stay with and get promoted, hopefully.

Good. What about your friends, do they work or study?

About half and half. Of my friends from university, half are doing postgraduate research, and the rest are in the workforce now, like me. We're earning some money at last!

And how do you stay in touch with your friends?

Just through social media, because we're spread all over the country now, and in some cases in other countries too. But we follow each other, and we see each other's updates all the time, so everyone knows what everyone else is doing.

What about your family, how do you keep in touch with them?

Well, I'm still living with my parents at the moment, so I catch up with them every day after work. My two sisters are much older than me and they live independently, and they come over at weekends so that we can all spend time together with them and their children.

What else do you like doing at weekends?

If the weather's good, I do a lot of cycling. I try to do two or three hours per day if I can, because I don't have time in the week.

Is that mountain biking, off road?

No, it's track cycling. There's an open-air cycle track in my town, which surprisingly is the size of an Olympic track, and I try to increase my speed and duration around it as much as possible. I have a racing bike, which isn't the highly advanced type you see in the Olympics, but it's very fast.

And what if the weather isn't so good?

In that case I watch movies. I like watching English language films with subtitles, because I find that helps my English. You pick up a lot of small phrases and bits of vocabulary that way.

Yes. What was the last movie you saw? What kind do you like?

It was 'The Many Saints of Newark,' which is an American gangster film. I like gangster films, generally speaking, because the plots are quite fast-paced and the humour is very entertaining. I think it's called dark humour.

Thanks for that. We've finished Part 1, and now I'm going to give you a card with a topic for you to speak about for between one and two minutes. You have a minute to prepare, and you can make notes if you wish.

Part 2

Task card

Describe something you bought which you were not happy with
Say what you bought and from where
Why you were not happy with it
What you did about this
And say what happened as a result

Candidate's notes during one minute preparation:

Big screen projector online, auction site, seemed cheap
Poor picture quality, noisy, start up
Complained to auction site, made official complaint, letter in post
Finally refunded, long wait, lots of trouble

Ok, so can you please talk on this topic for one to two minutes. Thanks.

So, I'm going to speak about a screen projector I bought last year. This is one of those projectors that takes an input and projects it, usually from a ceiling position, onto a white wall or screen to give a very large image. I mentioned a minute ago that I watch a lot of movies, and I wanted to fit this projector into our living room so that we could have a cinema type experience watching films and programmes. When they work properly, these projectors can give a high-quality image two metres wide, which is amazing. I bought this one in used condition from an online auction site, where people bid for an item on sale for a fixed period. I'd used this site before to buy some quite expensive stuff for cycling, and never encountered any problems with it, so I thought this would be pretty straightforward. At first it was, because I made the bid and the projector was despatched to me.

And that's where the problems began, because from the outset it didn't work properly. Even when you started it up, it took ages to start projecting, which is a sure sign that something's wrong with a projector either mechanically or in the software. I know all this because I researched online before buying it. Then, even when it was working, the picture quality was very poor, both the definition and the colour. These units should give an almost perfect definition, you see, like looking at a high definition TV screen, but this was blurred and fuzzy. Another problem was the noise it made, because it constantly whined and clicked while it was on, for some reason. Needless to say, it's very annoying if you're watching a movie and you get these noises overhead from the projector, which you're supposed to be able to forget about. All in all, there was no way I was keeping this thing and paying for it, because it cost me almost $900.

So, what did I do about this? Well, I complained to the seller who had shipped it to me, and I got no response apart from a standard acknowledgement. That was no good, so I complained to the auction site using their official complaint form online, which you might expect would get a quick reaction from them. Unfortunately, though, that wasn't the case, because they said they'd investigate, but again nothing actually happened. In the end, as I was faced with basically losing my $900, I wrote up a letter which threatened legal action against the auction site, and I sent it to them in the mail by recorded delivery, where they have to sign a receipt on delivery of the letter. That was so that they couldn't claim they never received it, which apparently is a problem in these situations.

The outcome of all this was that, a few days after they signed for the letter, I got a letter back from them in the mail. This letter said that, under the conditions of sale on the site, I was entitled to a refund but I would have to send the projector back at my own expense. Well, I could live with that, frankly, because the cost of sending it wasn't that great. So, I returned it and, a few days later, they emailed me to apologise for the delay and confirming that I was getting a refund, which I did finally receive onto my credit card shortly afterwards. That was a great relief, as you can imagine. I also noticed, because I was thinking of bidding for another projector, that the seller had been removed from the auction site, which was interesting to see. I suspect that there had been a lot of complaints about the items and the lack of response from the seller, and so they were taken off. In the end then, I managed to get this sorted out and resolved, but it was very frustrating for it to take so long, and it's ironic that it took an old-style paper letter in the mail to finally achieve that. I mean, it's ironic because it's a completely online company, which never sends out letters like that.

(The candidate spoke for approximately 2 minutes.)

Thanks. Do you still use this auction site at all?

Yes, I do, and I've never had any similar problems before or since this situation with the projector. I think it was what you might call a rogue seller, which is why they were removed.

And did you ever get another projector?

Yes, but I bought a brand new one online, from one of the major home entertainment sites. It's been absolutely perfect, fortunately, and we've had it running in the living room for almost a year now. Even if it goes wrong, it's got a three-year guarantee anyway, so I've got peace of mind.

I see. How did you know what to write in the letter about legal action?

I saw some examples online, and I asked a friend of mine who's a trainee lawyer about what I should say. Basically, you need to say that this is their final opportunity to resolve the matter before you take them to court, that's the idea.

Well, $900 is a lot of money.

Exactly. If it was $9, you might say, 'Oh, I'm too busy, I'll just leave it.' But with such a large amount, you have no choice really, you have to make sure you get it back.

Yes, well thanks for that. That's the end of Part 2, and in Part 3 now we'll discuss the topic of shopping generally.

Part 3

How can people protect themselves against crime if they're shopping online?

Well, that's a massive question, because there's so much fraud today resulting from online shopping. The obvious danger is someone stealing your credit card details, and that can be prevented by having security software on your device which stops people spying on the details you're submitting. It's absolutely essential to have that kind of protection. Another risk, and it's even greater, is a fraudster using your identity, with your name and address and so on, to pretend they're you and to take out loans or credit cards in your name. That's called identity theft, and it's a huge problem today. We can guard against that by using services which monitor the use of a name online, and the various financial details connected to it. Those two steps will go a long way to protecting anyone from online fraud and crime.

Thanks. Do you think that online shopping will ever replace physical stores completely?

In some ways that's already happened, I think. If we go around a town centre, we often see empty stores which used to sell things like household products or clothing, and they're closed down and shut for good now. That's almost always due to competition from powerful online retailers, because the prices are so much lower online, and getting next day delivery is actually more convenient than going into a town on the bus, or parking and so on. But on the other hand, stores such as supermarkets are still full of people today, even though they sometimes offer online ordering and delivery as well. And even shops which one might expect to be replaced by online retailing, such as bookshops, are still open and they're surprisingly busy. So, I think the replacement of physical stores by online stores has probably gone as far as it will go, at least for the time being.

Thanks. You mentioned supermarkets, do you think they're too powerful these days?

That's certainly a risk, that a group of large supermarkets might destroy smaller stores and then raise their prices and make unfair profits from the public. Anecdotally, when a supermarket opens in a town, people say, 'Oh, the little stores that have been here since grandma's time will have to close now.' And that does sometimes happen, which is a shame. But another side of this is that there's so much competition *between* the different supermarket groups. We see them fighting with each other to offer the lowest prices and the best value, and often consumers have a choice of two or three different supermarkets in their town, all competing with each other. So, I think that supermarkets becoming more dominant is a natural event, but, as long as they compete with one another and don't form a monopoly, the public can be quite relaxed about it.

Monopolies, you said. Are there any examples of shops forming monopolies which have damaged the public?

Well, I can't think of any in the supermarket world. But another example is in fast food, for instance. Often you'll see a town where one of the American fast food chains has opened two or three outlets selling burgers or chicken, and everyone goes to these places for their snacks, drinks and meals. This means that the traditional local shops, the coffee shops and snack bars and so on, these older places struggle and eventually close down because all their customers are going to the big chain stores. The town is then left with no choice or variety, apart from burgers or chicken or whatever it is. That's a real shame, and very unhealthy too.

Yes, I see. Now, imagine being the manager of a very large, very busy store. What skills would be needed?

That's certainly a tough job. I suppose, firstly, that a person would need to be extremely well organised, with excellent time management skills. That's because there must be so many issues to deal with at once, and new problems or crises are happening around you all the time during the day. So, this person would have to be very skilled at assessing problems and prioritising their time to deal with each one. At the same time, though, they'd need to be quite forward-looking and good at planning, because the success of the store relies on having the right staff available at the right time, and the right amounts of products to sell. Above all, I think a supermarket manager would need brilliant interpersonal skills, to constantly deal with their colleagues, all the staff, their own bosses, and the customers too of course, virtually around the clock. Those three characteristics are probably the most important.

Ok, thank you for all that. We've finished your test now.

***

Practice Test 4

Part 1

Tell me about your spare time interests. What are your hobbies or interests?
Why do you enjoy this activity?
What sports do you enjoy doing or watching?
Are you studying or working?
What are your plans for the next 12 months?

Part 2

Task card

Describe a meal or gathering you remember well
Say when and where this was
Who was with you
What happened during the meal or gathering
And say why you remember this so well

Examiner's follow up questions

Do you think you will have this kind of meal or gathering again?
How have you kept in touch with the people who were there?

Part 3

How should the authorities regulate restaurants?
Is food healthier today compared to the past?
How are eating trends changing today?
Do you think children should be taught to cook meals at school?

***

Practice Test 4: Candidate's Page ✂

The examiner should cut this page from the book and give it to the candidate in Part 2, but not before

Part 2 Task card

Describe a meal or gathering you remember well
Say when and where this was
Who was with you
What happened during the meal or gathering
And say why you remember this so well

Space for Candidate to Make Notes in One-Minute Preparation Time

Band 9 Example of Practice Test 4

In Part 1 now, tell me about your spare time interests. What are your hobbies or interests?

My main interest is the environment, and especially animal rights. I read a lot of media information about what's going on in the world, and I post actively online to my followers.

I see. Why do you enjoy this activity?

I think that people generally should be more aware of animal rights issues, especially endangered species. And the process of building up my number of followers is very interesting, so it's actually rewarding in itself.

Thanks. What about sports, do you do any or watch any?

Yes, I'm a keen swimmer at regional competition level. That means I represent my province in national competitions against other provinces. There's a major league table that we're all trying to win.

That's impressive. Why do you enjoy swimming?

It's a great challenge to swim against other people at my level, and I enjoy the competition. But I also like swimming for fun, especially in the sea near where I live. That's more about just being with nature and relaxing.

What are your plans for swimming over the next 12 months?

There's a big regional contest next month, so I'm in training for that. Hopefully my team will win that competition, and then we'll be in the national finals in the summer, if all the training pays off.

That's great. How does this fit in with your studies or work?

Well, I'm working part time at the moment for an animal charity on the fundraising side. That means I have enough spare time for training, otherwise it would be difficult to manage.

Have you finished your education?

I'm a qualified nurse, in fact, so yes that's all completed. There are further diplomas I'll need to get in order to progress in nursing, though.

And do you plan to work in nursing at some point?

I think so, in the long term. The problem is that it wouldn't leave any time for the swimming training, and all the trips to the competitions, so at some point I'll have to decide between the two. Not just yet, though!

At what point do you think you'll decide?

Probably in two years' time, when I'm twenty-five, and hopefully after I've won some national prizes for swimming. That's how I see it at the moment.

Thanks. Now we've finished Part 1, and for Part 2 I'm going to give you a card with a topic for you to speak about for between one and two minutes. You have a minute to prepare, and you can make notes if you wish.

Part 2

Task card

Describe a meal or gathering you remember well
Say when and where this was

Who was with you
What happened at the meal or gathering
And say why you remember this so well

Candidate's notes during one minute preparation

New York when I was 15, summer, heat, Central Park
Family, parents, brother, big holiday treat
Lost in the park, heat, feeling unwell, water!
Restaurant by lake, superb meal, unexpected, surprise

Ok, can you please speak for one to two minutes now.

This is about a meal I had a few years ago when I was fifteen. As my brother and I had done very well at school exams, our father took us and our mother to New York for a week for a special holiday. The four of us stayed in a very smart hotel, it was a real treat. So we saw all the sights, of course, and in addition to that, one afternoon we spent walking in Central Park, which is the huge open space in the middle of Manhattan. Now, New York in summer is very hot and humid, as no doubt you know, and on this particular day it was incredibly hot and uncomfortable. On top of that, the amount of pollution in the air was horrible. You could actually feel the pollutants swirling around, and to make matters worse, as we were walking around the park, we started to get a bit lost. It's a very big park, and the signposts aren't very helpful, and the four of us began to lose our bearings. We tried to use maps on our phones, but for some reason that didn't work, so we were wandering around in this really unpleasant environment, starting to feel quite unwell because of the heat and the terrible air quality. At one point, my mum almost fainted from the heat.

Then, as we were starting to get very stressed, we came around a corner on the path, and in front of us was a beautiful building in the shade of some tall trees, next to a lake where people were rowing in little boats. We realised this was a restaurant, and my dad said he would go in there and ask to buy some bottles of water so that we could keep going, and ask for directions too. But as we went into the lobby of this place, it felt really quite amazing. It had air conditioning and it was wonderfully cool, the air was clean, and the interior looked so calm and inviting. So, my father asked if they had a table available for lunch, and the staff showed us to a table on a kind of raised area, a gallery, looking out over the other tables and with a view of the lake. It was literally the best table in the whole place. We started to recover and really enjoy ourselves, and we ordered some food for lunch.

I have to say that this was some of the best food I've ever eaten. I remember there was a lot of seafood, with shellfish and grilled vegetables, and some delicious cold dishes as well. It was beautifully presented, with the cold food being brought on trays of ice and the drinks in buckets of ice, which of course was exactly what we needed. The atmosphere in the restaurant was wonderful too, because it was very calm and well-ordered after the quite stressful situation we'd been in outside. We were there for quite a long time, getting through this wonderful food and talking about the experience we'd had in the park. I remember that there was a person playing a piano at one end of the restaurant, and after a while we sort of settled back and just listened to this very nice piano music, and planning what we were going to do the next day. So, all in all, we were there for a couple of hours, I think, and the waiting staff were very friendly and relaxed about us sitting there and ordering desserts as the mood came to us.

The reason I remember this so vividly today is partly because of getting lost in Central Park and getting so hot and confused outside. That was a nasty experience which I wouldn't wish on anyone. But it's more because it was such an unexpected thing to happen, a twist of fate as they say. We didn't know that this lovely restaurant even existed, and, even when we discovered it by accident, we only wanted to get some bottles of water at first. And then to be offered the best table in the house, and to have such a nice afternoon recovering from our ordeal in the park – that was so unexpected and, of course, very welcome. We all felt very lucky indeed that we'd stumbled across this place in the way that we did. In some ways, it was both the low point and the highlight of our week in New York, the low point being getting lost in the park and the highlight being the lunch at the restaurant. My parents say that it certainly wasn't cheap, but it was definitely worth the price for such a nice memory.

(This candidate spoke for roughly 1 minute 45 seconds)

Ok, thank you for that. Do you think you'll go to that restaurant ever again?

Well, I'd love to go back to New York, so yes, I hope the restaurant would be on the list of things to do. Although some people say that places are sometimes disappointing the second time around.

I see what you mean. But you'd obviously recommend New York as a destination.

Oh, absolutely. And a week is probably the right length of time to see and do all the major things. I think that longer than a week would be a bit too much, because it's such a busy place and so crowded with people.

You mentioned your family there, do you still live with them?

Yes, I live at home. Our house is fairly near the swimming pool where I train, so it's an ideal location, and of course I don't have the pressure of taking care of the household stuff, so I can focus on my swimming and charity work.

Great. Well, that's the end of Part 2. In Part 3 now, we'll discuss the topic of food and diet.

Part 3

Do you think that food is generally healthier today than in the past, for example fifty years ago?

In some ways it probably is, yes. People today must be more conscious of the need for a healthy diet than they were fifty years ago, I think. For example, being a vegan or a vegetarian is very common today, whereas in the twentieth century it was apparently quite rare. There's also much more awareness of the dangers of fat and sugar, and the risks of foods that can cause cancer. Some of that is due to laws about food labelling, but also a general increase in our understanding of health. But on the other hand, if we look at many countries, there's a widespread problem with obesity, and that's something that was unusual in the twentieth century.

Was it unusual?

Well, yes . . . for example, when we see old films of people in the streets in the 1920s or 1950s, it's very noticeable that nobody is obese, which is certainly not the case today. And this is due to the low quality of junk food or fast food people eat today, and the huge intake of calories that many people think is normal. So overall, I think healthier food is certainly available today, but not everyone wants to benefit from it.

Thanks. You mentioned fast food. Why do you think so many people eat in fast food places?

Well, for various reasons. There's convenience, for one thing, because people have so little free time these days, and they can go in and have a meal quickly, or even eat in their car if they use the drive-through. There's also the question of value, because eating in a normal restaurant is quite expensive, and going to a fast food outlet maybe gives them the feeling of going out for a meal, but it costs much less. I think, from what I've read, there's another reason though, which is that the food itself is rather addictive. Apparently, there are certain additives in fast food products, like hamburgers, which release a feeling of happiness in the person eating them, because of the reaction in the brain. The person may not even be aware of it, but they want to experience that again, and they associate that feeling with buying another hamburger. By the way, that may explain how people become addicted to junk food as well. So, it looks like there are both conscious and unconscious reasons for these places being so popular.

Ok, thanks. Maybe it starts with education, do you think children should be taught to cook healthy meals at school?

I think they should, yes. It's important to teach them why certain foods and ingredients are healthy, and others aren't, and then to put all that together into how to actually make some dishes. Some schools combine this with subjects like biology and even budgeting, so the kids see how food and diet is connected to health and good finance. Of course, this needs to be carefully managed, so that it doesn't take up too much time in the school day, because cooking can be quite time consuming if you're doing it for the first time and learning as you go along. But as long as that doesn't become a problem, it's a very positive thing to do.

Right. What about restaurants, how should the authorities regulate them?

Regulating restaurants? Well, I certainly feel that's an important role for the authorities. First of all, there should be regular hygiene inspections, to make sure good practices are followed and the customers aren't at risk of getting food poisoning. The local authorities need the power to close down any restaurant that fails an inspection like that. There should also be compulsory fire safety inspections, of course, as well. What else? In some countries, the menus have compulsory information about the calories of each dish, and the percentage of a safe daily intake that it provides.

That's a good idea, so that people understand how many calories they're getting, and how much fat and sugar and so on. So, the authorities should make sure the food is hygienic, the building is safe, and also that the diners are informed about the dishes they're paying for.

Are there any disadvantages to having that information on the menu?

Well, possibly, in the sense that the food that's actually served on the plate may not match up with the details on the menu. The chef may be making it with a different level of fat, sugar or salt. That would be an obvious disadvantage. But, really, that's not a criticism of the menu information idea itself. It just shows that the information has to be accurate and reliable. In fact, that's another role for the authorities as well. They should check that the menu data matches what's actually there on the plate, by taking random samples or something like that.

Thanks. And that's the end of the speaking test.

***

Practice Test 5

Part 1

Tell me about your future plans for work, study and leisure.
Where do you see yourself in a few years' time, and doing what?
Do you plan to take any further qualifications?
What career would you like to follow? Why?
What are your leisure interests currently?

Part 2

Task card

Describe a time when you entered a race or competition
Say when and where this was
What the race or competition involved
What happened at the end of it
And say how you felt about this at the time

Examiner's follow up questions

How common is it for people to take part in an event like this?
What effect has this event had on you?

Part 3

Let's discuss sport and competitions. Why are big events so
popular?
Do you think the Olympic Games is a worthwhile event?
What qualities are needed to become a sports champion?
Can you think of any sports becoming less popular?
Do you think sports will change in the future?

***

Practice Test 5: Candidate's Page ✂

The examiner should cut this page from the book and give it to the candidate in Part 2, but not before

Part 2 Task card

Describe a time when you entered a race or competition
Say when and where this was
What the race or competition involved
What happened at the end of it
And say how you felt about this at the time

Space for Candidate to Make Notes in One-Minute Preparation Time

Band 9 Example of Practice Test 5

In Part 1 we'll talk about plans for the future. What plans do you have for the next twelve months, approximately?

Well, I plan to go to university in Toronto, in Canada, starting from October next year. That will be a three-year degree course in social and public policy, which is a subject I've always been interested in.

Why does that interest you?

It's a very varied subject, which can involve sociology, finance and also HR, that's human resources. People with this degree tend to go into the management of the public and state sector in Canada, for instance in the civil service or the education department.

Where do you see yourself in a few years? In Canada?

Probably, yes, if everything goes according to plan. I know several people who've followed this exact route, and now they're living and working in Canada. Once you've done that, you can always come back home, and employers here will be very interested in you.

That's good. Any idea where you'll live in Canada, at university and afterwards?

Well, at university I'll be on the campus in Toronto, which is a very nice location just outside the city. The campus has absolutely everything you could want: apartments, stores, sports venues, and plenty of restaurants for students. Oh, and lecture halls, of course.

Yes. Where would you live when you start work?

In Toronto or one of the other big cities, Montreal or Vancouver. That's where the big government departments are based, which I'll hopefully be working for. I've never actually been to Canada at all, but I've heard that the cities are very attractive places to live.

Will you need to take any further qualifications?

Possibly I'll need to do that, yes. There are some specific qualifications regarding the education sector, and others about legal issues in public administration. But I can do those while I'm working, as a part time course. I won't need to study full time again, as far as I'm aware.

And what about leisure, what sort of interests do you have now?

I like judo, which is a popular martial art, originally from Asia. I'm in my local club here, which is a lot of fun and very good for personal fitness.

Will that continue when you're in Canada?

Oh yes, there's a huge judo scene in Canada, they love it over there. It's not as big as something like ice hockey, which is their biggest sport, I think, although I'm not a fan of that particular sport. But judo's really very popular, and there'll certainly be a club to join, wherever I end up living.

Do you have any plans for what else you'll do in your spare time, if you live there?

Yes, I'd like to take up photography, and take pictures of Canadian animals out in the wild. I'd like to take pictures of those big animals, I think they're called elk, which live in the huge forests in Canada. That would be very interesting, and something really new and challenging for me.

Ok, thanks, that's the end of Part 1. For Part 2 I'm going to give you a card with a topic for you to speak about for between one and two minutes. You have a minute to prepare, and you can make notes if you wish.

Part 2

Task card

Describe a time when you entered a race or competition
Say when and where this was
What the race or competition involved
What happened at the end of it
And say how you felt about this at the time

Candidate's notes during one minute preparation

Environment challenge in high school, last year
National competition, eco mods to school building, planning and forecasting
Water collection system, growing vegetables
Came 5th nationally, very satisfied, feeling of success

Can you please speak now for at least a minute, maximum two minutes.

Yes, I'm going to tell you about a competition which I entered last year, during my final year of high school at the college here in town. The competition consisted of a national challenge open to all high schools, and the idea was for a group of students to design a modification to their school which would make the place more environmentally friendly. The way this worked was that within each school an initial contest was held, where several groups of three or four students each would propose a modification or an addition to the school building or the way the school operated, explain how this proposal would work, and forecast what environmental effect this would have. The students would vote for a winning group who would then build the design and enter the national contest.

For example, in my school, one group proposed adding solar panels and another group wanted to have a heat pump exchanger system for ventilation. Now, in my group, we were very conscious that the design had to be affordable and practical to implement, so we suggested a simple rainwater collection system which would irrigate and area of land behind the school which wasn't used for anything, and this piece of land would be cultivated. We proposed planting vegetables and fruit trees, so the food could be used for meals at the school. Our forecast was that, with very low output of energy, we could create consumable food where there was none before. We managed to win the nomination, so we went ahead and built the new system using donations from the students and their families, and a grant from the school itself.

Building the system was pretty straightforward, meaning we connected up pipes to the roof at one end and fed the water down to a flexible hose network in the ground. The difficult part was cultivating this plot of land which had been neglected for years. It was full of weeds, rocks and bits of old trash. We borrowed a mechanical digger and dug it all up, then cleared out the rubbish and added some fertiliser. The improvement was enormous once the water started to irrigate it, and we planted the vegetables and some fruit trees. To enter the national competition, we made a presentation about this online, and this was assessed and judged by the organisers centrally. We tried to emphasise the low cost and quick results of our modification, because the vegetables were going to be ready over the summer. In the end, we came fifth nationally, so we got a certificate and a, what would we call it? A plate engraved with our names, which was fixed to the wall inside the school.

As for how we felt about this, we were very pleased indeed. Our budget was very low compared to some of the other schools, who had designed complex projects like wind turbines which we would never have been able to do, either financially or with the know-how that we had. But the judges applauded us for having a simple scheme which had a direct benefit to the school, and they said this should be adopted by schools everywhere if the climate was suitable. So all in all, it was a very interesting experience, quite challenging physically, and with a great sense of achievement at the end. And I'm pleased to say that the piece of land is still being cultivated, of course, and the vegetables are taken directly to the school kitchen and used for meals. The fruit trees will take a few years to start to produce fruit, which we knew when we planned the whole project at the start.

(The candidate spoke for 1 minute 45 seconds.)

Thanks for that. How common are these competitions?

They run them every now and then, about every three years or so, I think. I imagine that funding would start to be a problem if it was done every year, because you'd constantly be asking the parents and schools for funds.

And what did you learn from this experience?

Well, some useful skills such as planning, both in engineering terms and financially, I mean knowing how much the whole thing will cost and who will pay for what part. I also learned the importance of networking and building up contacts to help with a project. For example, we borrowed the mechanical digger from one of the parents who has a construction company, and they supplied the digger machine and the driver for an afternoon. Having contacts like that is very important in life.

Yes, thanks for all that. Now we'll come on to Part 3, and discuss competitions and sport generally.

Part 3

Why do you think big sports events are so popular?

Big sports events being major football matches and so on?

Yes.

Well, for one thing, so many people grew up playing these major sports as children, whether at school or in the park or the street. So the vast majority of the population have been brought up with this interest, you could say it's in the culture around us. Added to that, the events themselves are usually very exciting and entertaining, even if you don't do the sport yourself. Most of us don't do athletics, for instance, but there's always a huge TV audience for athletics championships like the Olympics, because the races themselves are so exciting to watch. I think there's also the role of, what shall I call it? Group solidarity, maybe. I mean that people love to support a team or a player when they're watching with a big group of other people, in the stadium or at home. That's a reason why international football matches are so popular, for example. People know there are millions of other people cheering the team on as well, and that adds to the enjoyment.

Thanks. Do you think the Olympics are still a worthwhile event?

Well, I know they attract criticism these days, for all sorts of reasons. Some people say they cause too much disruption to the host country, which was the problem in Brazil for example, or that they're too expensive and the cost can't be justified. Other people say that drug taking by athletes makes the results unfair. But on the other hand, if an Olympic championship is carefully planned and organised, these objections become a bit less meaningful. As long as the costs don't get out of control, and provided the drug problem is eliminated, the Olympic games still make sense as an international event. I certainly wouldn't want to see them abolished.

Ok, thanks. What qualities would a person need to become a champion at that sort of level?

Well, physical qualities, first of all. They need to have a body suited to the sport, and they need to train intensively to achieve even tiny advantages over their competitors. They need to have remarkable flexibility and stamina to train so hard and to take part in the sport itself. For example, it only takes a few seconds to do a high jump, but the training is a round the clock programme, seven days a week. On top of that, though, there are the mental qualities. These people need to be incredibly determined, and be able to focus on the sport without distractions. They also have to be open to advice and criticism from their coaches and advisors. It's this combination of such unusual physical and mental abilities which makes someone into a champion, I'd say.

I see, yes. And how do you think sports will evolve in the future?

In the future? I suppose there may be new kinds of sports. For example, technology such as the suits people wear which let them jump out of a plane and fly through the sky, something like that might become a recognised competitive sport. It would certainly be exciting to watch. But overall, I'd say the future will be a series of small developments in the technology of existing types of sport. If you look at something like cycling, the bikes they use in the Olympics today are totally different from the bikes they had even a few years ago, because they're constantly being redesigned and improved. Even if we take something apparently simple like running shoes, small changes in the material of the sole can make differences of a fraction of a second. At the top level, that can make the difference between first place and third place, apparently. So I think we'll see a constant development of existing sports, making the athlete's performance just slightly better each time.

Ok, thanks for your answers. That's the end of the test.

***

Practice Test 6

Part 1

Tell me about your home town. What are the main employers?
What is the climate like there?
What do people do in their spare time?
Have you always lived there?
Would you like to live anywhere else?

Part 2

Task card

Describe a time when you worked with other people as a team
Say when and where this was
What you wanted to achieve together
How this team worked together
And say what the outcome was

Examiner's follow up questions

Have you worked in a team since then?
What did you learn from this?

Part 3

Let's discuss work and careers. What careers are the most popular
with young people today? What makes these careers popular?
What's the most important consideration when choosing a career?
Do you think working from home is a good practice? Why/why not?
How will careers and work change in the future?

***

Practice Test 6: Candidate's Page ✂

The examiner should cut this page from the book and give it to the candidate in Part 2, but not before

Part 2 Task card

Describe a time when you worked with other people as a team
Say when and where this was
What you wanted to achieve together
How this team worked together
And say what the outcome was

Space for Candidate to Make Notes in One-Minute Preparation Time

Band 9 Example of Practice Test 6

Part 1

Ok, for Part 1 now, please tell me about your home town or city. What are the main employers and businesses?

Well, my home town is way out in the countryside, so, as you can probably imagine, the main employers are the farms in the area. We grow a lot of sugar beet, and there are also businesses which process the beet and turn it into granules for transportation.

Where is it transported to?

I think it goes to large factories in the south, which use it to make food products. We always see large trucks carrying these granules driving south. That must mean the trucking itself is quite a big employer, actually.

I see, thanks. And what's the weather like through the year?

It's quite varied. The summer is reasonably warm, typically thirty degrees or so, but there's also a strong wind that's typical of the warmer months, so we don't get too hot. In winter it's very wet and windy, but spring comes quite early, and the weather in spring is just great.

What's it like in the spring?

Oh, it's pleasantly warm, with not much rain, usually blue skies, and quite warm nights as well. Everyone says that if the spring weather lasted all year, we'd have the best climate on earth.

That's nice. What do people do in their spare time?

To be honest, leisure facilities are quite limited. Older people do a lot of fishing in the rivers there, but there isn't much for younger people to do. That means we have to get the bus into the city nearby, to find things to do – especially in the evenings.

So, what is there to do in the city?

There's a good range of things on offer. There are cinemas, restaurants, night clubs and various sports facilities. Some people go in several times a week to train for sports or to see films, but personally I tend to just go in at weekends.

What do you do there, yourself?

On a typical day, I'll see a film, have a meal, probably do a bit of shopping, just that sort of thing. The stores that we have in my town are fairly basic and quite expensive, so if we want to buy anything apart from groceries, we go to the city where everything's much more modern.

I see. Have you always lived in your town?

Yes, I have, ever since I was born. It's a typical close-knit rural community, which in some ways is good, but in other ways people are always looking over other people's shoulders and trying to find out about their business, if you see what I mean.

Yes, I see. Would you like to live anywhere else?

Definitely. I've always imagined living in a big city, with so much to see and do, and so many people to meet instead of the same circle of friends all the time. I think I'd enjoy city life a lot, and I hope I get the chance to experience it.

Is there a particular city that interests you?

I'd like to go to Sydney in Australia, where the famous opera house is. But the visa requirements are quite hard to meet these days, apparently, so I'll probably try to live in London as a foreign student. I've seen so much of London in the movies that I almost feel like I know it by now.

Thanks for all that.

Part 2

Now we'll go to Part 2, and I'm going to give you a card with a topic for you to speak about for between one and two minutes. You have a minute to prepare, and you can make notes if you wish.

Task card

Describe a time when you worked with other people as a team
Say when and where this was
What you wanted to achieve together
How this team worked together
And say what the outcome was

Candidate's notes during one minute preparation

Painting outside of the house last year
Condition of the house, paint, weather, cost of paying someone
Organised buying paint, ladders, brushes, who did what
It worked ok, not perfect, better than before, nice to work together

So, please speak now for one to two minutes.

Ok, I'm going to talk about a time last year when my family decided to paint the outside of our house together. Our house is quite an old building, you see, and it's on top of a hill, so the weather has quite an impact on the exterior. The main walls of the house are made of solid stone, but they're surfaced with a smooth material which is typical of our region. I think the English word is 'plaster.' Anyway, that smooth surface has to be painted to stop it getting dirty or damaged by the sun and rain, and the last time it had been painted was around the time I was born, so that was almost twenty years ago. That's why, last year, my parents decided that it had to be repainted quite soon, because the existing paint was getting very faded and it was starting to fall away in some places. When that happens, the house starts to look very unwelcoming, and of course the plaster underneath gets affected by water.

Well, my parents looked into getting a professional painter to do this, but the prices they received from the companies they asked were extremely expensive. It's hard to see why it was so expensive, because the paint itself isn't a great expense, and it might take two people a few days to complete the work. So my father said, 'Let's do it ourselves, it can't be that difficult.' I have two brothers, you see, so there's five of us in the family including my mother. We saw this as a great challenge, because it was something we'd never tried before. It was the right time of year to do it, in early summer, so we all agreed to work together and paint the house. We decided democratically to choose a yellow colour paint. When I say democratically, that means my mother decided on it and we all agreed it was a good idea. It's traditional in our area to have a dark yellow paint which is a warm, strong kind of colour.

I took responsibility for buying the paint and the brushes and various other tools we would need. Oh, and also borrowing some ladders from other people in the town. The house is a single storey building, so we wouldn't have to go up very high to paint it. When everything was ready, we had a system where two of us would go along the wall getting it ready for painting by brushing the dust off it, and the others would walk behind us putting on the paint. When we finished a wall, we would all stand back and examine it, and if there were any areas to add more paint we would do that. Then we would put on a second layer of paint, with one person mixing the

110

paint and another person applying it. Then we'd go on to the next wall and repeat the process there. At the end of each day, we worked together to clean the brushes and tidy everything away to be ready for the next morning. In the end, it took less than three days to do the entire job, because after a while our system got faster and we became very efficient at painting and doing the second layer and so on.

And as for the outcome, for one thing we certainly saved a lot of money. We realised that the prices we were given for the work were just far too high, and we were glad we hadn't wasted money like that. As for the quality of the painting itself, I must admit it wasn't exactly perfect, because in some places the paint was slightly different colours. That must be because we put on too much or too little, or maybe we didn't clean the surface underneath properly first. But that only happened in a few isolated places, and you had to stand there looking at it for a while before you noticed. But overall, it made the house much smarter and more welcoming to look at, and of course it protects it against the weather too. One other outcome was that we found we really enjoyed working as a team, with each person knowing what to do and playing their part nicely. It was very satisfying, and you could say it brought us together even more as a family. It's something I'd definitely recommend to other people, this idea of doing a project together as a family, especially if it's something connected to your house or apartment. It's a very enjoyable way to spend a few days.

(The candidate spoke for 1 minute 50 seconds.)

Thanks for speaking. Have you done any other projects like this?

We haven't done anything as major as this since then, no. But we have been thinking about building a swimming pool behind the house, which obviously would be a huge operation in itself. I think for that project we'll have to get the professionals in, though, because it would be too complicated for us by ourselves.

Yes, sure. What work is involved in building a swimming pool?

Well, imagine all the digging, and then all the pipes and the electrical connections, and those filters and special chemicals that the water needs. We wouldn't know where to start with all of that, and if you get it wrong it could be highly dangerous, of course. You could poison yourself or get a lethal electric shock. We could certainly design it ourselves, for sure, but then we'd have to give the design to experienced people who know how to do it.

Thanks, and that's the end of Part 2. In Part 3, let's discuss work and careers.

Part 3

What careers are the most popular with young people today?

The most popular careers? Let me think a moment. Well, a lot of young people want to be lawyers or accountants, so those two are certainly very popular. It does seem, though, that not everyone who wants to follow those careers actually manages to achieve that, because the qualifications are challenging and can be difficult to get. Another career that inspires a lot of young people is finance, meaning that they would work for a bank or an investment company, for example. But now that I think about it, those careers are the traditional, conventional ones. These days there are alternative careers which a lot of young people follow, such as being an influencer through social media, or creating your own content for sites which can be monetised. In some cases, those activities are even better paid than accountancy or law, and of course they're much less stressful and demanding of your time. So, there are some conventional careers which are still popular, and some new types of careers which are also in demand, but for very different reasons.

Thanks. What do you think are the most important things to consider when deciding on a career?

Well, I think most people would agree that a main priority should be enjoying the work. We spend so much time and energy at work that, if someone doesn't enjoy it, they become demotivated and depressed. So, job satisfaction should probably be top of the list. Having said that, people do need to think about the financial side. Having a job that doesn't provide enough money to live the lifestyle you want is also quite depressing, as many people are finding these days. So, a second consideration is definitely the salary potential. I'd say a third aspect is lifestyle, actually, meaning what effect this career will have on your personal life and where you need to live. A lot of people want to be doctors until they realise they have to be available at short notice and live in a city near a hospital, for example. So overall, people should think about job satisfaction, the salary, and the impact on their life. Ideally, you can find a career which ticks all of those boxes for you, if you're lucky enough.

Thanks for that. A lot of office workers are working from home these days. Do you think that's a good practice?

Well, from what I've heard, that's a trend which started a few years ago, but it really caught on during the pandemic when people had to self-isolate. In some ways it can be a positive way of working. For example, it does away with the need to commute, which saves a lot of expense and cuts down on the pollution a person causes by travelling to an office. It also allows the worker to focus on tasks without distractions like gossip or chatting at the water cooler and so on. But on the other hand, a lot of companies now are stopping people working from home, and they're doing that because working in an office as part of a team is actually very good for the staff and for the organisation. People bond together better, they come up with ideas together, and discussions face-to-face are more authentic than over a video link. And for the individual worker, being at home all day can be very isolating and depressing, especially if your home isn't suitable for desk work. So, overall, I side with those people who say home working is not such a great way of doing things. I think people benefit from being in an office environment, and so does the employer at the end of the day.

Thanks. How do you think careers will change in future?

I think we're already seeing one of the really major changes, which is the rise of Artificial Intelligence at work. Companies and public sector organisations are using AI in ways which will potentially make very large numbers of white collar workers redundant. In fact, law and accountancy, which we were talking about a minute ago, are types of work which could be done by AI very easily. The same is true of many public administrators, by which I mean people working for government departments and local authorities, for example. I think that in the near future we'll probably see the end of those kind of managerial jobs as a career, because, after all, the AI system doesn't need vacations or sick pay or a pension fund, so the cost savings to the employers will be absolutely enormous. Obviously, there'll be a need for people to oversee the AI, but that requires far, far fewer workers.

What do you think will happen to all the redundant workers?

Well, that's a good point, because putting all these people out of work overnight would have a very destabilising effect on society. Some of them will find positions working alongside the AI, or managing it, but I guess the vast majority will need to find other ways of making a living. It's interesting that skilled manual work, such as plumbing or electrical work, can't be replaced by AI, because the physical movements can't yet be automated by robots. So maybe those careers will grow in popularity and demand.

I see. Interesting. Well, that's the end of the speaking test now.
***

Practice Test 7

Part 1

Tell me about your home country. What is the climate like?
What are the main festivals?
What sports are popular?
Is there a national dish and/or a national costume?
Which are the main cities and/or visitor destinations?
How do people travel around?

Part 2

Task card

Describe a test, exam or assessment you remember taking
Say when and where this was
How you prepared for the test
What you did in the test
And say what the result of the test was

Examiner's follow up questions

What did you learn from this experience?
What advice would you give to other people taking this test?

Part 3

Let's discuss education generally. What are the qualities of a good school?
What skills are needed to be an effective teacher?
Is it important for young people to go to university? Why/why not?
Do you think workplace training is a good concept?
How will new technology change education in the future?

***

Practice Test 7: Candidate's Page ✂

The examiner should cut this page from the book and give it to the candidate in Part 2, but not before

Part 2 Task card

Describe a test, exam or assessment you remember taking
Say when and where this was
How you prepared for the test
What you did in the test
And say what the result of the test was

Space for Candidate to Make Notes in One-Minute Preparation Time

Band 9 Example of Practice Test 7

Part 1

Let's talk about your home country. What's the climate like?

Well, it's a tropical country, so the climate is very warm throughout the year. We don't really have clearly defined seasons as other countries do further south or north, but we do have a rainy season in October. The rain is essential for agriculture, and for maintaining the water supply.

Thanks. What are the main festivals?

There's a huge independence celebration in May, when everything stops for two days at least. There are parades and various official ceremonies, but generally people take the chance to have parties and family get-togethers. That's the time when we all see our distant relatives and friends we haven't seen for ages.

What sports are popular?

The national sport is football, and that's definitely the most popular sport for people to watch and take part in. But a lot of people also like volleyball, which has become really popular over the last few years, so that's probably the second major one.

Why do you think volleyball is getting so popular?

We have a few key players who are very important figures to a lot of young people. They're influencers as much as players, I suppose you might say, and they've made volleyball very fashionable with both men and women. So, it's been driven by their personalities and their popularity.

Thanks. Is there a national costume?

Do you mean for volleyball, like a sports kit?

No, sorry, I mean generally, a cultural costume.

Oh, I see. Well, there's a traditional floral dress which ladies wear on special occasions, like the independence parades and that sort of thing. For men, there's a traditional type of hat, but that's mostly for the older generation now, to be honest.

I see. And what are the main visitor destinations?

The capital city must be the main tourist destination, I think, although I've never actually seen any statistics about that. There's a series of large parks and squares which are very impressive, you might have seen photos of them in fact. There's also a port on the Pacific coast which is very beautiful indeed, and a lot of visitors try to see it if they can.

What's beautiful about that city?

There's a harbour with old buildings from the 19th century which are very well preserved. The whole harbour looks almost like a movie set, and in fact it's been used for filming a lot of movies and TV series over the years.

I see. And how do people travel around inside the country?

The main transport system is the road network, which is very well looked after. For longer distances there are regional airports, and we have two domestic airlines which cover the routes between the main cities.

Is there a train system?

We're a bit unusual, because we don't have a train network, apart from some small metro type systems inside the big cities. That's because we have a lot of mountains and ravines, so the landscape would make building proper train lines between cities much too expensive and complicated. Or at least, that's the reason the government gives, anyway.

I see, thanks. That's the end of Part 1, and now in Part 2 I'll give you this topic card. Please prepare for a minute, make notes if you wish, and then speak to me for one to two minutes.

Part 2

Task card

Describe a test, exam or assessment you remember taking
Say when and where this was
How you prepared for the test
What you did in the test
And say what the result of the test was

Candidate's notes during one minute preparation

Scuba diving test last year in coastal resort
Two weeks preparation, practice, planning, using equipment
Written test, 30 minutes diving, surfacing
Now qualified as scuba diver

Please start speaking now for one to two minutes.

I'm going to talk about a test I took last year, in July to be exact. This was a scuba diving test, which is an internationally recognised assessment that classes someone as a competent scuba diver who can dive unaccompanied and also look after inexperienced divers if needed. I did this at a coastal resort in my country, which is a venue that's well known for diving, and I attended a specialist scuba school with really expert trainers. By the way, I should maybe have said that the word scuba is an acronym, meaning self-contained underwater breathing apparatus, which refers to the tanks of air which divers carry on their backs to allow them to stay underwater for long periods of time. There are obviously big dangers involved in doing this activity, so being properly trained and qualified is essential. Otherwise you run the risk of drowning or being permanently disabled through what's called oxygen starvation.

Well, this diving school which I went to offered a full two-week training course, where they take you from being completely inexperienced to being qualified. As you can imagine, this was a very intensive course, because we were training and practising every day, with only one day off in the whole two weeks. There were ten of us in the class, and we were taught, first of all, how the breathing apparatus works, and how to check that the air tanks are properly filled for the length of dive you want to make, and of course how to breathe through the mouthpiece which feeds you the air. Incidentally, the gas in the tanks is compressed air, not pure oxygen as some people might think. They also trained us in planning a dive, which means how to make sure that the water you're diving into is safe and free of obstacles which might trap you. Then of course we were taught how to enter the water properly while wearing the tanks on our backs and the flippers on our feet, and how to move around underwater in an efficient and safe way. All of that may sound simple, but it's vital to have an instructor explain all of this and talk you through it. When you're underwater, you see, even a small mistake can have very serious consequences. In fact, part of the training included how to recover from mistakes and how to rescue other people who might get into difficulties.

Coming on to the test itself, this consisted of a written test, first of all, where we had to show that we could calculate things like the amount of air needed for dives of different lengths and depths, and how to do the filling of the tanks safely. There were also questions about safety regarding boats or ships that might be passing nearby while you're underwater, which is another danger in this sport.

Once we passed that exam, we went on to a practical assessment, meaning that we showed the instructors we could put on the equipment correctly and operate it ourselves. This involved diving off a boat into the sea, and swimming underwater to a certain depth and making a series of actions. All the time we were observed by the instructors who were watching for mistakes or for ways that people didn't perform the tasks properly. Then finally, of course, we had to surface properly and show we could get back onto the boat and handle the removal of the equipment correctly. This all took about thirty minutes, which is quite a short time considering it took us two weeks to get ready for it.

And the result of the test was that I passed, fortunately. I say fortunately, because a couple of people on the course failed it and had to take it again afterwards. This means I'm now a qualified scuba diver at a basic level, and I'm allowed to hire my own equipment and dive on my own if I want to, although it's not recommended to dive alone at this basic level. It certainly gave me a great sense of achievement to pass the test, especially as the course was so intensive. The other outcome of the test is that it should help my application to join the coastguard in my country, which is the service, obviously, which rescues people from ships in difficulty. That's always been an ambition for me, and, after my studies abroad are finished, I'll come back and apply to join them.

(The candidate spoke for 1 minute 30 seconds.)

Thanks. Why would you like to join the coastguard?

For some reason, I'm not really sure why, I've always liked the idea of rescuing people. It's an important job and a very interesting one. My friends tease me and say I should be a lifeguard instead, who is the person on the beach like in Baywatch, if you've seen that movie.

I see. And what advice would you give to other people taking this test?

Well, probably *not* to do it as an intensive course. It takes the fun out of it a bit, if you know what I mean. It makes it a bit too stressful and rushed, when really diving should be an enjoyable and relaxing kind of sport, if it's done properly. I'd say, do the test certainly, but build up to it over a few months or even a year if you possibly can.

Thanks for that, we've finished Part 2 now. In Part 3, let's discuss education generally.

Part 3

Thinking of schools, what are the qualities of a good school?

Well, there are several important qualities. For one thing, it needs to be a safe and supportive environment, where the pupils or students aren't worried about any dangers or risks. It's very sad that these days there's a lot of violence in schools, and the education authorities need to take steps to stamp that out. For another thing, the staff need to be very knowledgeable and expert in the area they're teaching. Having an expert teacher is very motivating for students, I think we'd all agree on that. I'd say there's another quality too, which is encouraging the students to have interests which aren't just academic. So, a school should have a full programme of activities outside of the lessons themselves. I think the term for that is extra-curricular activities. So those three things are the essential qualities, I'd say.

You mentioned teachers, what other skills are needed to be an effective teacher?

In addition to being knowledgeable? Well, a good teacher needs to be very patient with the students, because not all of them will progress at the same rate, and the ones who are slower need to be encouraged and helped. An effective teacher also has to be a very good communicator, meaning they can get ideas across to the pupils and answer their questions efficiently. I suspect we've all had teachers in the past who talk for hours without really communicating much. Actually, another skill is being able to keep discipline in the class, but without being too strict or severe. That's a skill in itself, and it's probably something that good teachers develop over time, while others never quite manage it.

Thanks. Do you think it's important for young people to go to university?

Well, there are two sides to that question. On the one hand, everybody should be encouraged to have the highest level of education they can achieve, which for many people does mean going to university. It's also the case, I think, that university graduates tend to earn higher salaries in their careers, which is important of course. But on the other hand, doing a degree is very expensive in itself, and in many cases the person ends up doing a job they'd be able to do without a degree anyway. So, in some cases, going to university can be a waste of time and money at an important stage in your life, I'm sorry to say. So, on the whole, I think it can be important, but it's not essential by any means. It depends what someone's long term plans are, and whether they can really justify all the cost and the years of study. That's what people should ask themselves.

Do you think workplace training is a good concept?

Meaning getting qualifications while working at a job?

Yes.

I'd say that's a very positive thing, very positive indeed. In a lot of ways, it gives someone the benefits of having a salary and progressing their education at the same time. It's even possible these days to do a degree while you're working, which would solve some of the problems I mentioned a minute ago. And from the employer's point of view, it lets them get the most out of their people in the long term, by building up their qualifications while contributing to the organisation through their work. I suppose the cost of these programmes has to be considered carefully, because you can't have absolutely everyone in an office taking time off for studies or exams and so on. But I'm sure employers will factor that in when they're deciding whether to offer it to their staff.

And what about the future, how will new technology change education generally in the future?

Well, the big advance in technology which will change education is definitely Artificial Intelligence. Using AI in classrooms, which I think will start to happen at scale very soon, will allow schools to tailor lessons to the needs and interests of individual students. So instead of a teacher standing at the front of the class delivering one standard piece of information to everyone, which is the way it's been done for hundreds of years, we'll see students interacting individually with an AI teacher. That means the AI will start to understand the knowledge and learning ability of each individual student in a school, and teach them in a very personal way. Some people say that the role of the teacher will change from being an expert at, say, maths or history, and become an expert at showing the pupils how to use AI to learn about maths or history. I hope that makes sense the way I've described it. It'll be a real revolution if that happens.

Well, thanks for talking. That's the end of the test now.

***

Practice Test 8

Part 1

Let's talk about your studies. Where did you go to school?
What exams have you taken?
Why did you take those exams in particular?
Do you have plans to study further in future? Why/why not?
What about your friends, what are their plans?

Part 2

Task card

Describe a time when you bought something expensive
Say when this was and what you bought
Why you decided to buy this thing
From where you bought it
And say whether you were pleased with your purchase

Examiner's follow up questions

Have you bought anything else like this?
What suggestions would you give to someone considering such a
purchase?

Part 3

Let's discuss money and finance in general. Do you think it's better
for people to save money or to spend it?
Why are some people wealthier than other people?
Do you think governments should decide salary levels?
How can countries become more prosperous economically?

***

Practice Test 8: Candidate's Page ✂

The examiner should cut this page from the book and give it to the candidate in Part 2, but not before

Part 2 Task card

Describe a time when you bought something expensive
Say when this was and what you bought
Why you decided to buy this thing
From where you bought it
And say whether you were pleased with your purchase

Space for Candidate to Make Notes in One-Minute Preparation Time

Band 9 Example of Practice Test 8

Part 1

Let's talk about your studies. Where did you go to school?

I went to a small school in my home town until I was eleven, and then I attended a much bigger school in a nearby city up until the age of eighteen. Luckily for me, both schools were actually very good, and I had lots of friends in each one.

Thanks. What exams have you taken?

Well, I took a series of basic exams when I was sixteen, which we call the school leaving tests, covering all the main subjects. Then I did the IB or international baccalaureate exam when I was eighteen, which is equivalent to a high school or pre-university test in other countries.

Why did you take those exams in particular?

The school leaving tests are required by the state, so I had no choice about what to study, unfortunately. But in the IB exam, I selected certain topics which are interesting for me personally, such as history and music.

Why do you find those subjects interesting?

I like history because of the perspective it gives us on past events, figuring out how things happened even though people at the time maybe didn't understand what was going on. That's fascinating. And I like music because I've always played the piano, and in the long term I'd like to be a professional singer.

What kind of music would you sing professionally?

I could be what's called a backing singer, who adds vocals to someone else who's singing the main part. That would get me into the music industry, which is a very difficult business to break into, because it's very competitive.

Yes. And do you have any plans to study further in future?

I'm hoping to go to university in America or Britain, or one of the other English-speaking countries. I have a friend who's at a university in Colorado at the moment, in America, and I'd like to follow that kind of pathway.

What's your friend studying?

It's interesting, she's actually doing forensic criminology, which is the study of crimes and gathering evidence. Personally, I wouldn't want to do that, because it's highly technical, but we have interesting conversations about the techniques she's learned and how the police would use them.

Interesting. What's she planning to do in the future?

She says she wants to stay in America, then get citizenship and join the police there. That's a big challenge, of course, because of all the requirements, but she's very determined.

Thanks, that's the end of Part 1. Now I'll give you this card, please prepare for a minute and then speak for one to two minutes.

Part 2

Task card

Describe a time when you bought something expensive

Say when this was and what you bought
Why you decided to buy this thing
Where and how you bought it
And say whether you were pleased with your purchase

<u>Candidate's notes during one minute preparation</u>

My bike, 2 years ago, wanted a bike for getting to school, cycle tracks
Previous one stolen, budget from parents
Researched different types, reviews, visited bike store, tried several
Good bike, but a few problems (brakes)

Ok, please start speaking now.

So, I'm going to speak about my bicycle, which is something I bought two years ago. I've always had a bike ever since I can remember, and I really enjoy cycling. It's also very good for your health, of course, which is another reason why I like it so much. Well, a few years ago I had a very good quality bike which I used for getting to school. The local authorities built a cycle track across the countryside from our town to the city, so you can cycle all the way there without having to go on busy roads at all, which is brilliant. But, unfortunately, that bike was stolen from our house when I stupidly left it outside without locking it. It's a sad fact that a bike which is unlocked will just disappear, even in a small town like ours.

Well, that was a setback for me, because I was so fond of the bike and because I loved riding it on the track to school. So, my parents managed to claim some money from their insurance company for the theft of the bike, and using that they gave me a budget to go out and buy a new bike. The budget was a bit less than the value of the stolen bike, but I was pretty sure I could get a good replacement by choosing the right model really carefully. So, I read up on the different models that were available in that sort of price range, and I thought about which one was going to be the best for me. I needed a combination of factors, meaning a bike that can be used on roads but also on the cycle track, which can sometimes be a bit uneven and muddy. That meant I didn't want a mountain bike as such, but I did want a versatile model that could go from track to road. In the end, I decided on three possible models, and I went to a cycle store in the city to look at them up close.

This bike store was incredibly helpful, in fact. They even ordered in one of the models that they didn't have in stock, just so that I could try it. I think that's an excellent commitment to customer service, by the way. This meant that, when I went in to the shop, I could take a proper look at each of the three bikes, one after the other. They were all fairly similar in design, with a few small differences which could be quite important. For instance, one of them had heavier tyres than the others, while another one had a slightly different set up of the gears. The third one had a much bigger frame, what you might call a heavy-duty frame. These differences might sound small, but, when you're using a bike every day, they can make a big difference to how you use it and how effective it is for you personally. All of these small points has to be considered because it's tempting to make a rushed choice, but then you'll regret it later on. In fact, the bike store had an area outside where people could try out riding the bikes before buying. It was a flat, level area like a car park, so not like reality I suppose, but at least you could feel how the bike behaved when you started to ride it. I tried each of the three bikes for about ten minutes each, and that let me evaluate the differences and finally choose the best one. The one I opted for was the one with heavier tyres, because I thought they would work well on the cycle track and still be fine for using on asphalt in the streets.

Now, I'm well aware that some people would do all this and say 'Thankyou' to the people in the shop, and then go home and buy it online. Personally, I don't like doing that, because I think it's unfair to the store staff who've been so helpful and made such an effort for a customer. Especially in this case, where they tried really hard.

It was slightly more expensive buying from the store, but I think that's perfectly reasonable, considering they have to pay for the sales team and the premises and so on. So, in the end, I bought the one I wanted from the store and took it home the same day. As for whether or not I was pleased with the purchase, I have to say that generally I was pleased, and I definitely felt I'd made the right choice. The bike was just right for the trip to school, and it was great around town as well. I had a few small problems with the brakes, which weren't adjusted quite correctly, but I took the bike back to the store and they set them up again so they worked perfectly. So all in all, it was an expensive purchase but a successful one, and I'm glad I bought it from the shop and not online.

(The candidate spoke for 1 minute 40 seconds.)

Thanks for that. Do you still have the bike?

Yes, and I still use it regularly. I go to work by bus these days, because I can't turn up all muddy from using the track. But I use it at weekends, and I definitely think I'll be keeping it for a few years into the future.

What advice would you give someone thinking of buying an expensive bike?

Well, first of all do your research, like I did. There are so many forums you can read where people give reviews and opinions on the latest bikes, so you can benefit from their experience. Another thing is, do you need to buy it brand new? You could get one that's a couple of years old and has been well looked after, and it'd be like having a new one from the factory, really. And it would be quite a lot cheaper. That's an important point to consider.

I see. Well, that's the end of Part 2, and now for Part 3, let's discuss money and finance in general.

Part 3

For example, do you think it's better for people to save money or to spend it?

Saving versus spending? Well, that's a difficult choice for many people, isn't it? I mean, saving is important because people should have some money in reserve in case of problems in life such as illness or accidents. It's also a way of making sure you aren't at the mercy of your employer in case you have a disagreement with them, which can easily happen. But on the other hand, life is for living, and people should enjoy themselves as much as possible, which often will involve spending money if you can possibly afford it. There's no point being miserable if you have lots of money in the bank at the same time. Overall, I would come down on the side of spending, I think, as long as you have just a bit put away for emergencies.

Thanks. Why are some people wealthier than other people?

That could be for a variety of reasons. Some people are lucky enough to inherit money, or to have a rich family that supports them. Or it may be because the person is highly qualified and earns a high salary, or even because they've had a great business idea which has been very profitable for them. But of course, where you live in the world makes a huge difference as well. By that I mean that people born into wealthy countries will almost always be better off than people born in poorer countries, just because of the size of the economy they're living in. So, I suppose being rich could be due to hard work, or it could just be luck a lot of the time, depending on the individual situation.

Do you think governments should decide workers' salary levels?

In some cases, that already happens, for instance when people work for the state as civil servants or as the police and military and so on. In almost every country, I think, those salaries are decided by the government. That's absolutely correct, I'm sure, because the government knows how much to pay in order to get the right people and keep them in the post. But that's only half the story, because of course there are all the private sector workers who are employed by companies or who work independently. In those cases, their salaries should be decided by their employers, or by themselves if they're self-employed. I really don't think it would work if a government starts trying to set salaries for supermarket workers or farmers. Unless, of course, the state is the owner of the supermarket or the farm, which might be the case in some places. All in all, though, I think private sector pay levels aren't a matter for the government of the day at all.

Thanks. How can countries become more prosperous economically?

Well, it's certainly the case that there are huge differences in prosperity in different countries around the world. You don't need to be an economist to see that straight away. I don't know enough about the topic to be really sure of what the reasons are, but I imagine some of it is to do with certain countries having established industries a long time ago and keeping ahead of their competitors. Maybe the watch and clock industry in Switzerland is an example of that. But one way for a country to improve its economy is probably to invent new technologies and new processes, and export those ideas to other countries. Governments can help with that by welcoming in inventors and designers who can create these things, and providing a stable environment for them to work in so that they can produce things that the world needs. As I say, I don't know enough about the subject to be confident, but that seems like a good place to start.

I see. What sort of new technologies could be the next big thing, maybe?

Oh, I don't know . . . maybe something to do with generating electricity in a clean way even when renewable energy is at a low point. For instance, if it's night and there's no wind, how do you generate electricity without fossil fuels, if you have no hydro-electric source? There's a lot of talk about small electricity generators which can power a street or even a single building, and these generators can work off a new type of power which is completely safe and can't possibly go wrong like the old nuclear reactors. Some people say the fuel will be hydrogen or helium, which are completely harmless to handle and store close to you. I think the country that finally invents something like that and can sell it around the world will become incredibly prosperous, and of course it'll make a huge contribution to human progress.

Thanks for speaking. That's the end of the test now.

***

Practice Test 9

Part 1

Tell me about your hobbies and interests. What do you do in your spare time?
Do you do any sports? Why do you enjoy this?
What interests do your friends and family have?
Are there any sports you'd like to do in the future?

Part 2

Task card

Talk about a film, movie, TV series or book you especially like
Say what this is and what is in it
When and where you watched or read it
Why you like it
And describe any changes you would make to it

Examiner's follow up questions

Do you know anyone else who likes this?
What other movies, books etc do you like? Why?

Part 3

Let's discuss movies, TV programmes and books generally. What types are popular at the moment? Why are they popular?
Do people read books less today than in the past?
What effect have audiobooks had on people?
How will books and movies/TV etc change in the future?

***

Practice Test 9: Candidate's Page ✂

The examiner should cut this page from the book and give it to the candidate in Part 2, but not before

Part 2 Task card

Talk about a film, movie, TV series or book you especially like
Say what this is and what is in it
When and where you watched or read it
Why you like it
And describe any changes you would make to it

Space for Candidate to Make Notes in One-Minute Preparation Time

Band 9 Example of Practice Test 9

Part 1

Tell me about your hobbies and interests. What do you do in your spare time?

When I get some free time, I like to play badminton with some friends, which we do at a court we can hire near to where I live. It's a really nice afternoon, because we'll play a few games, then have a coffee and relax, and walk outside if it's warm.

Why do you enjoy badminton in particular?

It's a very skilful game, and when you play it with four people there's a lot of teamwork and sort of reading the other person's mind, if you know what I mean. That's how you win, by having an intuitive understanding of what your partner will do next.

Thanks. Do you have any other interests?

I listen to podcasts a lot. I'm interested in wildlife preservation, and there's a huge variety of podcasts available to listen to about that, especially by animal experts and environmental commentators. I like to listen when I'm on the bus or just at home by myself.

What interests you about wildlife?

I've always liked animals, and my family has always had pets - not just normal pets, but also chickens, goats and even sheep. That started my interest, and now I'm very concerned that a lot of species are going to become extinct because of human behaviour.

Yes. Where do your family keep the animals?

There's a field behind our house which is ideal for keeping them. It's quite a lot of work, because the chickens have to be checked every day, and the sheep need a lot of attention at certain times of year. The goats are more independent-minded, though.

I see, thanks. What other interests do your friends and family have?

My friends who play badminton also go go-karting a lot. That's a small car that goes around a track for fun, I'm sure you've seen them. I've tried that a few times, but I don't like it so much because it's incredibly noisy. I go just to keep my friends company, really.

What about others in your family, what do they do in their spare time?

Well, my brother is a motorbike fan, so he's always fiddling with his bike and riding it around with his friends in a kind of gang. Not a crime gang, though, just a fan club for motorbikes. My parents are very different, they're great chess players, so they go to a lot of chess tournaments all around the country.

Are you a chess player?

I do play, but I think that chess is one of those things where it's easy to be fairly good, but it's very difficult to be very good, if you see what I mean. It's a bit like tennis, some people say, where almost anyone can be quite a reasonable player, but not many people can rise above that level. I've never been able to rise to an exceptional level at chess, I mean a competitive level where you can play in tournaments.

Thanks. Are there any different activities or sports you'd like to do in the future?

There's a thing called bungee jumping which I'd love to do. It's the sport where you jump off a high platform on an elastic line, and you bounce up and down. I'd really like to do that, but you see some tragic stories where people have had accidents, and that's put me off a bit.

Yes, I can understand. Well, we'll come on to Part 2 now, and I'll give you this card. Please prepare for a minute, making notes if you want to, and then speak on the subject for one to two minutes.

Part 2

Task card

Talk about a film, movie, TV series or book you especially like
Say what this is and what is in it
When and where you watched or read it
Why you like it
And describe any changes you would make to it

Candidate's notes during one minute preparation

Game of Thrones series, Based on a book, idea of the story, the world, places, characters
Watch it with friends or alone, fun times
Very exciting, dramatic, unexpected events, amazing characters
Want another series

Please start now.

Well, I'm going to speak about a TV series which ran for a few years called 'Game of Thrones.' This was an incredibly popular series, at least it was in my country, where people watched it as soon as new episodes were streamed, and you often heard people talking about it. For example, on a bus or train, you'd hear people saying, 'Wow, I saw episode five yesterday, it was superb,' and they'd have a discussion about it. It won lots of awards as well, so it must have been popular in other countries too. I think it was made in America or Britain, and it was based on a book which had been published a few years beforehand.

The idea of this series was that there's a world which looks a bit like Europe maybe seven hundred years ago, where people fight with swords and spears, and there are aristocratic families and peasants. But this world is very strange, because it's divided into seven kingdoms which are all fighting and competing with each other, and inside each kingdom there are noble families who are all competing to have power over each other. This means there's a continuous cycle of battles and fighting between the families, who sometimes form alliances with each other and then start fighting again. It may sound repetitive, but what makes it so interesting is the characters who lead the families, who are all remarkable people with special talents and also huge problems in their lives. I think one reason it was so successful is that, although the characters are wearing these old costumes and living in castles, they behave and talk a lot like modern politicians, because they're always plotting and planning to undermine each other at every opportunity. Sometimes you literally don't know what they're going to do next.

I tended to watch this series either with a group of friends in the evening, or sometimes alone on my tablet. To be honest, I watched each episode several times, which gives you some idea of how exciting it was. If I saw it with friends, sometimes we used to cook a meal which looked like the food the characters would eat in 'Game of Thrones,' and a few times we'd dress up in clothing that was meant to look like their costumes. Once I made a helmet out of kitchen foil so it looked like a knight in the series, and someone else would wear a raincoat like a cloak, and so on. It sounds silly now, but at the time it was so much fun.

As to why I liked it so much, well I've mentioned the excitement of the story and the way the characters are very exotic but also strangely like us in the modern world and our own politicians. I think the phrase is 'double cross,' when you make a deal and then betray the other person anyway. That's happening all the time in their world, and it really keeps you on the edge of your seat. But on top of that, most of the characters are very appealing, even though they're so ruthless and deceitful. So even when one of the evil characters is killed, you feel rather sorry for them because you secretly liked them. Also, the way the series was filmed was amazing. The scenery and the sets were incredibly imaginative and high quality, just as good as movies like 'Lord of The Rings' or 'Harry Potter,' for example. Everything about the series was very impressive, from the story to the acting and the camera work itself.

So, would I change anything about it? I think the only thing is that it ended too soon. There were eight series in all. Most people wanted another series, but in the end that was impossible because the characters literally all killed each other in the final episodes, until only a few were left. I really would like to see a sequel to it, or maybe what they call a prequel, which shows you the events before the story started. I think that would be fascinating, and I'm sure there'd be an enormous audience ready to watch it, because so many people enjoyed it the first time around.

(The candidate spoke for 1 minute 25 seconds.)

Ok, thank you. Have you read the book it's based on?

Actually, I haven't. That's because I'm not a great reader of books, really. Maybe I should try listening to the audiobook, but I think that might be a bit disappointing after seeing all the images on the screen.

Do you think you'll watch it again?

Yes, definitely. When I get the chance, I'm going to do what they call binge watching, where you watch a whole series of ten episodes in one weekend, for example. I think that'll be a lot of fun, and it'll remind me of all the enjoyment I got from it the first time.

I see, ok. That's the end of Part 2, and now in Part 3, let's discuss movies, TV programmes and books generally.

Part 3

What types are popular at the moment?

Do you mean what types of movies and so on?

Yes. And why do you think the popular ones are so successful?

Well, thinking of what you see on the streaming sites at the moment, there are always lots of action movies high in the rankings. Those are movies or series which feature lots of shooting and crime, for example with bank robbers or spies. Those kinds of stories have always been popular, I think, because people get the chance to see things they would never witness in their normal lives. Or at least I hope they wouldn't witness that. There are also lots of documentaries which get very high viewing figures. These are programmes which investigate something in the real world, or they're reporting on something important in society. People watch them because they give an informative view of something we didn't know about before, and that's a satisfying feeling to have. When you think, 'That was interesting. I'm glad I found out about that,' it's almost as if you've achieved something new.

Are there any other very popular types?

Well, another type of movie that's very popular is the fantasy type, which involves imaginary kingdoms, often with monsters or magical events going on. The appeal of the fantasy type is that it lets people into a world that's completely different from what they know. Having said that, as I mentioned about 'Game of Thrones,' part of the experience is that the people often resemble people we know today. So, I'd say that action, documentaries and fantasy are probably the most popular kind of movie or tv series today. They're certainly the ones that are always high in the rankings, anyway. I don't know about books, though, because, as I said, I'm not really a book reader.

Thanks. Do you think people read books less today than in the past?

I'm not sure about that. It may seem to be the case that people aren't reading books, because, for example, if you go to a public library these days it's usually virtually empty. The same is true of bookshops, which seem to have very few customers even at busy times of day. But the reason for that may also be that people are reading books on electronic devices, which is a very popular way to read now, instead of on paper. That's true of newspapers too, by the way. Oh, and of course they may also be listening to the book as an audiobook, rather than reading it off the page. So, I think before we can say whether reading books is becoming less common, we'd need to see some statistics on the ways people are using books, meaning how they're accessing the book. They may be consuming them, but in a different way than before.

You mentioned audiobooks, what effect have they had on people?

Oh, I think they've had a real impact. It's not necessary to sit still with a book in your hand in order to absorb the ideas or whatever is in it. People can listen to a book while they're travelling, for example, or while they're exercising or doing something around their home. So that lets you access a book just as you would with a podcast. That means people can continue to enjoy books even with a very busy lifestyle, or if they don't like sitting still for long periods of time. It also means that people who don't like reading for some reason, or who have trouble with reading as well, all these people can get the benefit of a book without having to actually read it. It's likely that for a lot of people who wouldn't be able to read a book, audio has made a big difference to their lives.

Yes. And how will books, movies and series change in the future?

I think the basic types of these things will stay the same, I mean the classic types like fantasy, action, horror and so on. I think the word for that is genre, so the genres will remain. But as for movies, I think we'll see the graphics reach a level where they can replicate a human actor so well that nobody can tell the difference. I think within a decade the major films will have graphic actors alongside humans, and the graphics may even replace human actors completely. The cost savings to the film studios would be huge, and it would allow them to invest even more in the graphic technology. We might get to the point where movies are created entirely on software, but the audience watching can't tell the difference between an AI actor walking down a street made by graphics and a human actor in a real city street.

Are there any negative aspects to that?

Well not everyone will be happy with that, obviously, and not just the actors. A lot of people who like movies will be uncomfortable at first with not having humans in them at all. But then after a while, I think people will forget their doubts and start to enjoy the movies for what they are. Just like when the cinema first started, films were silent and black and white, and now we've moved on a long way. Maybe not everyone liked movies with sound at first, but then they got used to it and began to appreciate it.

Thanks. What do you think will happen to all the actors?

Well, that's a good question. Unfortunately, I think acting might become something just for the stage in theatres. I think the household name actors might go into creating the movies, so when you go to see a Margot Robbie movie, for instance, it means she's designed it and directed the software, not that she's personally in it. But I think the days when a major movie has three big human stars and dozens of other human actors – those days are probably coming to an end soon.

Interesting, thanks. Well, that's the end of the speaking test.

***

Practice Test 10

Part 1

Let's discuss your home country. What dishes are popular to eat?
If people have vacations, what do they tend to do?
Would you like to visit or live in any other countries? Why/why not?
Do people in your home country keep pets or animals?
Do you have a pet or an animal?

Part 2

Task card

Speak about a person you know who is important to you
Say who this person is
Why they are important to you
How often you meet or keep in touch
And say what you talk about with this person

Examiner's follow-up questions

How will you keep in touch with this person in future?
What other people do you have a good relationship with?

Part 3

Let's discuss families and friends generally, not yours in particular.
In general, what changes to family life have happened over recent years?
How do people keep in touch with friends these days?
What are the advantages and dangers of using social media to keep in touch?
Can we be friends with someone without ever meeting them?

***

Practice Test 10: Candidate's Page ✂

The examiner should cut this page from the book and give it to the candidate in Part 2, but not before

Part 2 Task card

Speak about a person you know who is important to you
Say who this person is
Why they are important to you
How often you meet or keep in touch
And say what you talk about with this person

Space for Candidate to Make Notes in One-Minute Preparation Time

Band 9 Example of Practice Test 10

Part 1

Let's talk about your home country. What are the most popular dishes to eat?

Well, we grow a lot of rice for domestic use and for export, so traditionally most of our dishes contain rice in one way or another. These days, though, people have started replacing the rice with things like pasta or potatoes, just for variety I think.

Is fast food popular?

You mean, places like burger takeaways?

Yes.

Oh yes, they're very common in the large towns and cities, especially in the town centres. People go into them to grab something for lunch especially, whereas in the past they might have gone home to have a meal with their families. Out in the countryside they're less common, though.

Thanks. If people have vacations, what do they tend to do?

People tend to have short vacations at home or visiting relatives, which is a big part of our culture. In a typical year, we'll go and visit relatives probably ten times, which shows how important it is to us.

I see. Do you have a big family?

At home it's just my parents, myself and two of my sisters. But we have a huge extended family which is scattered all over the place throughout the country, so we spend a lot of time travelling to visit them so that we keep in touch.

How do you travel?

It's mostly by car, but if it's a long way we'll go by plane. That works out to be very expensive, though, as you can imagine I'm sure.

Yes. Do people in your home country keep pets or animals?

Traditionally, people have always had cats in the family home, and our older relatives still like having lots of cats around. But keeping birds is also very popular, I mean colourful birds like parrots which can be kept indoors a lot of the time.

Do you have a pet or an animal?

We have a family cat, who we've had for years now, so he's pretty elderly. My sisters have a few fish which they look after in a tank, but that's too complicated for me to enjoy.

Why is it complicated keeping fish?

Oh, you have to look after the water in the tank, adding chemicals to it and keeping it clean and all of that. Sometimes they'll spend a whole afternoon cleaning the tank and changing the water, and that's too much for me.

I suppose they enjoy it.

Well yes, it's a hobby for them, and they like keeping the whole thing really fresh and clean, which I admire them for. But sometimes I go out with my friends for the afternoon, and when I get back they're still working on the fish tank, and I think that's taking up too much of their time.

I see. Thanks, that's the end of Part 1 now. In Part 2, I'll give you a topic card to speak about for one to two minutes. You can make notes for a minute first.

Part 2

Task card

Speak about a person you know who is important to you
Say who this person is and how you know them
Why they are important to you
How often you meet or keep in touch
And say what you talk about with this person

Candidate's notes during one minute preparation

My best friend Rusanna, started school together, lives near me
Lots of interests in common, music, art, sense of humour, families
are close
See her few times a week, socialise, play music, jogging
Talk about plans (moving away) work and future

Ok, can you begin now please.

Well, I'm going to speak about my best friend Rusanna, who is very important to me for all sorts of reasons, which I'll explain. She's exactly the same age as me, and I've known her since we were small children and started at nursery school together. We would have been four years old then, and we're nineteen now, so obviously that's almost all our lives. Because, you see, after nursery we then went to school together and then to the same high school as well. On top of all that, she lives near me in our town, so we've always done things together in our free time as well as going to school together. The funny thing is that she looks a bit like me, or we look like each other, so a lot of people think we're sisters. Sometimes people don't believe us when we say we're not related at all, and they say we're playing a joke on them.

Thinking of why she's important to me, for one thing we have lots of interests in common. We both like enjoy similar music, and we both play the same musical instrument, which is the guitar. In fact, we've thought about forming a duo and putting out some music, and maybe we'll do that in the future. Another interest we share is art, because we both really appreciate the work of impressionist painters from the nineteenth century. We often go to the art gallery in the city to see some of the paintings which are on display there, and, every time we go, we seem to find something new to look at in the paintings. On top of that, we share the same sense of humour, which means we both enjoy some of the big American comedians that stream shows. Another thing is that our families know each other very well, and we often socialise with them, especially in the summer when it's warm and we have barbecues together. So, as you see, there are lots of reasons why she's important in my life.

As for how often we get together, it used to be every day when were at school, because we used to walk or take the bus there together. These days because we're both working it's less often, so in a normal week we might meet up two or three times, including the weekends. We often go to a café for an hour or so and catch up with each other's news, or go to my apartment or hers and play our guitars for a while. We've written quite a few songs together by now, which is why we'd like to make it available on streaming. We also go running together sometimes, because we have similar stamina and we can pace each other effectively, which is a great way to keep fit.

So, what do we talk about when we meet up? Well, apart from all the usual news and gossip, we often talk about our future plans. That's because we're both planning to move away soon. She's going to university and I'm planning to move abroad to get work experience in an English-speaking country. Naturally, that's a huge step for both of us, because we've never lived away from our families before. In fact, now that I think about it, we've probably never gone for more than a couple of weeks without seeing each other too. So it's going to be a completely new phase of our lives, and it'll certainly be difficult to get used to, at least at first. But we like talking about all the new places we're going to see over the next couple of years, and imagining what life's going to be like with so many new people and new things to do and so on. We also discuss what kind of work we'll end up doing and whether we will eventually move back home. So, we have a lot to talk about, as you can imagine.

(The candidate spoke for 1 minute 25 seconds.)

Thanks for that. How will you keep in touch with this person in future?

Through social media mostly, I'm sure, plus the occasional phone call, probably. We know each other so well that we can share news and thoughts very easily through messaging. It must have been a lot harder to keep in touch in the old days when there were only phones and letters.

Sure. What other people do you have a similar relationship with?

There's a little group of us who went to school together, and we're all constantly in touch with each other to keep up with what everyone's doing all the time. You can get a good idea of what someone's doing just by looking at their latest pictures. But Rusanna is the only one that I meet up with in person so often.

Thanks. That concludes Part 2, and now in Part 3 we'll discuss families and friends generally, not yours in particular.

Part 3

In general, what changes to family life have happened over recent years?

Well, I think the long-term trend is that families are getting smaller. That's a trend that's been going on for decades, in fact since the early twentieth century, I believe. The effect of that is that the individual children may get more attention from their parents, and they may have more resources devoted to them in terms of time, diet and finance. Of course, that doesn't necessarily make them happier, but it probably makes them healthier and better educated than children living a hundred years ago. But in more recent times, another change to family life has been the increasing level of divorces between married couples, which in some countries is over 50%. That means that very large numbers of children live with one parent, or with what are called blended parents, where they've remarried with someone else. So overall, there's a combination of fewer children but also less predictability and stability about their parents' marriages.

Do you think this is a global trend?

Global meaning worldwide? Well, I haven't seen any statistics for the complete world situation, but I suspect that this trend is being repeated in almost all countries in the world. I do believe that, generally speaking, children are healthier than they were in the early twentieth century, which is partly due to there being fewer children within each family and better diet and healthcare being available to them. And I also suspect that most countries have made it easier and quicker to get divorced than, say, a hundred years ago when it was apparently very complicated. So, even without any data, I would say cautiously that yes, this is probably a worldwide trend.

Thanks for that. What about friends, what are the advantages and dangers of using social media to keep in touch with them?

The biggest advantage is that people don't need to write letters or make phone calls to be constantly aware of what their friends are doing. So, we can be instantly updated about their plans and what they're doing, minute by minute if that's what a person wants. A lot of people like this, because it lets them keep in touch with large numbers of friends or followers, which would be impossible without internet programmes. On the other hand, though, these platforms can lead to a range of problems because of the pressure they create for people to appear popular and have lots of followers. They can also lead to issues such as bullying and even identity theft, so people have to use them carefully. All in all, I think most of us would agree that the benefits of these platforms make them worthwhile, as long as the users are conscious of the risks, and guard against the dangers.

Thanks. Can we be friends with someone without ever meeting them? Is it ever the same?

Well, it's true that meeting them personally lets you see the other person's reactions, behaviour and general demeanour a bit more clearly than talking to them online, whether that's on a video call or on social media. And the interaction between you and that person will be a bit more spontaneous, maybe. There's also the fact that you can be doing things with them while talking to them, like having a meal or some other activity. But on the other hand, the difference is there but it's not that great, really. The only thing that might be missing is the ability to be doing an activity with them, but if the person is a long distance away, you wouldn't be able to do that anyway. That means you might as well have a friendship with them online, because otherwise you wouldn't know them at all. So I think it's not exactly the same, but it's fairly close in most respects.

Ok, thanks, and that's the end of your speaking test today.

***

Practice Test 11

Part 1

Let's talk about your spare time interests.
Where do you follow your interests? How much does it cost?
Do you do this alone or with other people?
Why do you enjoy this interest?
What other interests do you have?

Part 2

Task card

Speak about a time you made or built something with your hands.
Say when and where this was
What you made or built
Why and how you did this
And say what happened to the thing you made or built

Examiner's follow up questions

Have you ever built something similar?
What did you learn from this experience?

Part 3

Let's discuss how things are made. Do people prefer things hand-
made, or produced in factories?
How have factories changed, compared to the past?
Do people still want to work in factories? Why/why not?
What kind of jobs have replaced factory jobs?

***

Practice Test 11: Candidate's Page ✂

The examiner should cut this page from the book and give it to the candidate in Part 2, but not before

Part 2 Task card

Speak about a time you made or built something with your hands.
Say when and where this was
What you made or built
Why and how you did this
And say what happened to the thing you made or built

Space for Candidate to Make Notes in One-Minute Preparation Time

Band 9 Example of Practice Test 11

Part 1

To begin, let's talk about your interests. What do you do in your spare time?

My main interest is flying kites, which I know is a bit unusual but I enjoy it enormously. I fly kites almost every weekend, if the weather allows, which means it can't be too rainy or extremely windy. The conditions have to be moderate.

What kind of kites are these?

They're stunt kites, which are large very flexible kites designed to move around quickly and smoothly with small inputs from the flyer, that's the person controlling them. I have three of them, and I choose which one to use depending on the conditions on the day.

Where do you do this?

There's a wide-open space in the hills, about half an hour away by car, which is ideal. I don't like to use a public park or gardens, because there are too many people around most of the time.

Why does that matter?

Well, for one thing, people come up to you and try to start conversations about the kite, and that's a distraction. Another thing is that you mustn't be near buildings or electric cables, because, if the kite comes down and damages them, you can be liable for the repairs. And, of course, the wind tends to be better out in the countryside.

Do you fly them alone?

Well, that's an interesting point. I'm in a kite club which meets now and then, very informally really. But there's not much you can do alongside other people flying kites. I mean, you can't race them, for example. So, most people fly them alone, like me.

Isn't there a tradition of fighting kites against each other?

Yes, in some countries people fight them by trying to cut each other's lines with blades on the kite. That must be fun, but they're specially-made disposable kites. I couldn't do that with my kites, because they're too expensive to replace.

Can I ask how much they cost?

Sure, I don't mind saying. They're about two hundred dollars for a good quality one, so as you can see, I couldn't lose one every week.

Yes. And why do you enjoy this interest?

Well, there's the challenge of making the kite do what you want to do in the changing conditions, which is a lot of fun. But more than that, you feel sort of connected to nature while you're flying it, because you can feel the power of the wind, and of course you're looking up at the sky all the time.

What other interests do you have?

The other thing I do is go bowling a lot. That's a very different activity, because you're always with other people and it's very sociable, as you probably know. That means it's a big contrast with flying the kites, which is quite solitary, but I enjoy them both very much.

So, you go bowling in a group?

Oh yes, bowling on your own would be quite boring. I'm in a team, and we play against other teams in the town once a week at least. It's a very loud and noisy evening, and very satisfying if you beat the others.

Well, we've reached the end of Part 1 now. In Part 2, here's a topic card to speak about for one to two minutes. You can make notes for a minute, then speak.

Part 2

Task card

Speak about a time you made or built something with your hands.
Say when and where this was
What you made or built
Why and how you did this
And say what happened to the thing you made or built.

Candidate's notes during one minute preparation

Science class, age 15, school, Mrs Toniati
steam engine, loose pieces
a puzzle, team work, everyone involved
It worked, school assembly, still there today?

Okay, please start now.

Well, I'm going to talk about a time I built something in a science class when I was fifteen or sixteen. At the time, I really enjoyed science lessons at school, because we had a very interesting science teacher called Mrs Toniati, who I remember very well. Quite honestly, the secondary school I went to wasn't very challenging in terms of the other subjects, but in science this teacher made everything very enjoyable and interesting to do. She was very keen on getting the students to make things for the various experiments and pieces of research we did, so we always felt involved and we were always busy. In one lesson, which was about atmospheric pressure, she told us that a great way to see this in action was to see a steam engine working. 'Well,' we said, 'a steam engine? Nobody has had one of those for hundreds of years, have they? Have you got a video to show us or something?'

But she then presented us with a big box of parts, which it turned out were the parts of a small working steam engine, which was just like a real one, except it could fit into a table. Our task was to put all the pieces together so that it worked, but without an instruction book or anything to show us how each piece worked and how it all connected together. At first, it was too confusing, because a lot of the parts looked similar and we had never seen a real steam engine working, obviously. But after a while, we put the larger pieces together, and then we figured out how some of the other pieces fitted in, so it all became clearer as we went along. I remember, especially, that everyone in the class got involved in this, by which I mean that nobody was hanging around at the back and not paying attention, which often used to happen when there was a group project going on. Everyone was making suggestions and trying to work out how the final pieces fitted together. In the end we got it finished and the whole machine actually worked.

This is where I can tell you what happened to this thing I helped to build, which is that we managed to start it and get it running. This meant we had to fill part of it with water, and another part which had the heater we fitted a small gas cylinder into. Then, by activating the burner which heated up the water, this steam engine got up to working temperature and the cylinder began to move up and down, which in turn made the wheel go around. This may not sound very exciting, but to us at the time it was a major event because we had built it ourselves.

We also took it to a school assembly, which is a session where the whole school comes together to hear notices and so on, and demonstrated it up on the stage in front of all the other pupils. By the way, in the end we took it to pieces again and put everything back in the box where it was kept, so that the next year's class could use it and benefit from it in the same way. Apparently, this was done every year as part of the final science lessons, so that steam engine had been through several generations of students, and I'm sure it was put together and taken apart by many classes after us. It's probably still there, being started up by a new class right now, although maybe with a new teacher, because Mrs Toniati was getting towards retirement age, even back then. So you could say the steam engine has been very good value for money for the school in the long run.

(The candidate spoke for 1 minute 30 seconds.)

Thanks for that. How big was this thing?

About a metre long, so it fitted on a table, as I mentioned. I didn't move around on wheels, though. It stayed fixed on the table and the wheel span around to show how the system worked.

I see. Have you ever built something similar?

No, I'm not mechanically minded at all. I'm the last person anyone would ask to help build an engine or something like that. That's why the steam engine lesson was such a success, I think, because even the pupils who weren't technically gifted all played a full part.

What did you learn from this experience?

Well, apart from the scientific angle, I learned not to reject something just because it seems old fashioned or obsolete at first. Obviously, they're old machines, but the lesson about atmospheric pressure is sort of timeless, you could say.

Okay, I see. Now let's do Part 3, and we'll discuss the way things are made or built.

Part 3

Do you think people these days prefer their products to be hand-made, or produced in factories?

Well, that would depend on what the product is, I think. I mean, some products are more valuable because they're hand-made by experts with a high level of skill. For instance, a hand- made watch or hand-tailored clothes are seen as very desirable things to have, because there's a suggestion of expertise and care in the way they're produced. The same goes for food, I think, because you might see in a restaurant a menu that says 'our hand-made spaghetti' or something like that, and it sounds more special. But that only applies to a few types of products, really, because most things don't need to be hand-made at all. And of course, there are some products we wouldn't want to be hand-made.

That's interesting, what would we not want to be made by hand?

Well, for example, if you heard about a hand-made phone or a hand-made laptop, that would seem a bit strange to most of us, because I'd expect those things to be mass produced in a factory. It wouldn't seem more special, it would seem kind of out of date or obsolete. Maybe what we're saying is that very traditional items like watches or jackets have extra value by being hand-made, but technology products don't, because the technology involved means they should be made through automated processes, for instance by robots rather than human workers. There's a word in English which I think is 'artisan.'

Can you explain more?

I think an artisan is a craftsman or skilled worker in a traditional setting. I say that because I saw an advert recently for 'artisan bread,' and it was incredibly expensive because it's made by some kind of expert baker. That sounds lovely, and we'd all like to buy artisan bread or an artisan watch. But an artisan computer wouldn't make sense, because we don't expect computers to be made by a craftsman.

Ok, I see. And how have factories changed compared to the past?

Well, for one thing, they're safer than in the past. It used to be very dangerous, working alongside huge machines and handling dangerous chemicals and so on. Deaths and injuries in factories used to be quite common in the twentieth century, I think. But there's another difference too, which is that there are fewer people working in them at all. Because so much manufacturing is automated, we just don't need large numbers of people involved in the process. So, for example, if you see an old photo of a car factory, it's full of people clustered around the cars with their tools, even if the cars are on a production line. But today, it's full of robots, and there's just one person in an office watching them on a tv screen. It's a remarkable difference, and pretty unfortunate for those workers who lost their jobs along the way.

Do you think people today still want to work in factories?

In many cases, yes, I think so. For example, the person I mentioned in the car factory who monitors the robots. That's a skilled and important role, and lots of people would be interested in doing that, I think. On the other hand, the kind of factory work where people operate machines all day in a repetitive way, I think fewer people would want to do that than in the past. But, as I said, there are far fewer of those jobs available today, anyway.

What kind of jobs have replaced factory jobs?

What's replaced factory work? Well, probably administrative roles in offices, where people are crunching data and reports. We can also say roles like call centre jobs, where people are answering phones for long periods of time. Those jobs can't be automated, at least not yet. But that may happen too, in fact, by linking Artificial Intelligence to an artificial voice. Then the companies wouldn't need to pay the administrators or the call centre staff, and unfortunately the workers would be out of work all over again.

I see, thanks. Well, that's the end of the test now.

***

Practice Test 12

Part 1

Let's talk about your home town. What's it like?
What do the buildings look like?
What do people do in their spare time? In the day/the evening?
What do your friends do for work/for leisure?

Part 2

Task card

Speak about something you use regularly to make your life easier
Say what this thing is
What you use it for
When and how you use it
And say how this makes your life easier

Examiner's follow up questions

Is this thing expensive to use?
Would you recommend this to other people?

Part 3

Let's discuss things people use in daily life
What machine or device do you think is most important in everyday life?
How is life different from 100 years ago?
What new inventions will arrive in the future?
How will this affect our daily lives?

***

Practice Test 12: Candidate's Page ✂

The examiner should cut this page from the book and give it to the candidate in Part 2, but not before

Part 2 Task card

Speak about something you use regularly to make your life easier
Say what this thing is
What you use it for
When and how you use it
And say how this makes your life easier

Space for Candidate to Make Notes in One-Minute Preparation Time

Band 9 Example of Practice Test 12

Part 1

Let's begin with your home town or city. What's it like?

It's quite a small town, and it's positioned halfway between two very large cities, so there are a lot of people living there who work in the cities and commute in every day. That means it's becoming more like a suburb of the cities these days.

What do the buildings look like?

Well, there's an old central part, where the buildings are from the nineteenth century. But the rest of the town is quite recent, with concrete and glass buildings and modern apartments. It's a big contrast, really.

What do people do in their spare time, generally, during the day?

We have a football team which has a big following locally, so a lot of people go to the stadium to support them at weekends. Well, we call it a stadium, but it's a pretty basic football ground, to be honest. But thinking about it, the whole town is quite empty on weekdays, because everyone's out at work.

What about in the evenings?

There's a big street in the old part of town which has a lot of cafes and restaurants, so people go there in the evening sometimes. It's quite expensive, though, so it's more for special occasions than regular eating. Oh, and there's also a lake which has a lot of food vans and kiosks dotted around it. That's much better value, and the food is actually very nice.

How often do you go to the lake?

Me, personally? Once or twice a week, probably. I tend to go there with a group of friends, and we sit by the water and eat something from one of the vans. It's a low-key kind of evening, but it's still enjoyable, at least in good weather.

Do your friends work or study?

Most of them are busy working, either in the big commercial centres in the cities, or in the town itself. Some others are still studying, but most of us have finished that stage and we're starting to build careers, hopefully.

What kind of careers are your friends following?

It's quite varied, because some of them are in retail, training as store managers, while others are working as accountants or some kind of office job. I have one friend who's in the army, but we don't see much of him because he's away on duty a lot.

Did you ever consider doing that?

Joining the army? Well, I wanted to join the air force as a navigator on a plane, but unfortunately my eyesight without my contact lenses isn't quite good enough. They said I could apply to be a technician on the ground, but I decided against it in the end. If I'm going to be on the ground, I might as well be a civilian.

Thanks, and let's start Part 2 now.

Part 2

Task card

Speak about something you use regularly to make your life easier

Say what this thing is
What you use it for
When and how you use it
And say how this makes your life easier

<u>Candidate's notes during one minute preparation</u>

Honda bike, describe it, powerful, bought it from a friend
Commuting, best of all worlds, cheap and fast
Describe commute to and from work, timings, safety conscious
Makes life easier, saves time, saves money, compare to car or train

Ok, can you please talk for one to two minutes now.

I'm going to speak about an item I use regularly, which is my motorbike. It's a Honda, but I won't go into all the details of the exact type, because it might get a bit complicated. I'll just say it's quite a large, powerful bike which you need to be a fairly experienced rider to handle safely. In fact, I bought it quite cheaply from its previous owner, a friend of my family, because he had crashed it and injured himself by not being able to ride it properly. He decided not to risk it a second time, so I had it repaired and fixed up to run like new again. I keep it in the secure parking space underneath the apartment building where I live, which is important because otherwise they get stolen quite easily.

Anyway, the main use I have for this motorbike is commuting into the city for my work. The options for getting into the city are either on the train, or by bus or private transport, and the train or bus are unreliable and surprisingly expensive. That's why most people go by car, but as you can appreciate that produces a lot of congestion, and traffic jams are very common. So I have the best of both worlds, in some ways, because I have my own independent transport but I can also drive past all the stationary cars and get to work faster than anyone else.

As for when I use it, I get the bike out every morning at around seven thirty. I have a full bike protective suit which I wear for riding, which basically helps protect your spine and skin surface from injury if you do crash or fall off, which fortunately has never happened to me. And I have a helmet, of course, so all this takes a few minutes to put on. I carry my work clothes in a container on the back of the bike, called a pannier. So by around seven thirty-five I'll be riding out of the apartments and starting to go through town, which is getting busy even at that time of day. To get to the motorway that leads to the city, there's just one main road, so it's almost always packed with cars. But I'm able to move past the cars quite quickly and get onto the motorway in a fraction of the time it takes the car drivers. Of course, I'm very careful about road safety and avoiding any possible accident. Being on a bike, the consequences of having even a small accident can be very serious, as you can imagine, and I'm very conscious of the risks of riding. So I don't weave in and out between cars, for example, I just keep a steady progress past them all, and then get onto the motorway itself. That's another advantage of having a bike, because the cars have to wait in line at a toll booth, but bikes go straight through without waiting, so I'm saving time and the price of the toll. Then, on the motorway, I'll make even faster progress because there's more room to go past the cars and trucks, and generally I'm at work in the city by around eight fifteen. To give you some idea, the same trip by car would get me there around nine am, probably. At that point, I change into my work clothes and store my bike suit in the pannier, and the bike is locked up in the car parking garage at work for the day. In the evening, I do the journey back the same way, but one thing I've learned is that the traffic is more dangerous in the evening than in the morning. In the morning, all the car drivers are in a hurry to get to work, but going home they're all tired and bad-tempered, and I have to be even more careful not to have an accident. I usually get home around six thirty, and put the Honda away for the night.

Travelling like this makes my life easier in a couple of ways. For one thing, it obviously saves me a lot of time compared to any other way of commuting, whether by car or train. I'm literally going door to door in half the time a car would take, and without having to get to the station and hang around waiting for a train. That's important to me, because it means I get a bit more sleep in the morning and more free time at the end of the day. The other advantage is that it costs very little compared to the other options, because it's got very low fuel consumption and there are no toll charges or train fares. That means I can enjoy my leisure time more, because I have a reasonable amount of spending money left over from all the other bills I have to pay. So, all in all, I'm very pleased with my Honda, although of course it's not something that would suit everyone.

(The candidate spoke for 1 minute 55 seconds.)

Thank you. What do you do in the city?

I'm training to be a specialist electrician, which means I deal with the circuits in air conditioners and heating systems in tall buildings. It's an interesting job, because it often involves trouble-shooting problems and trying to fix them without causing too much disruption to the people using the building.

How long have you been doing that?

Just for a year, since I left high school. It'll take another year to qualify, and then I can either stay here or move abroad and do similar work there. There's a lot of demand for these skills, and my company is recognised as a global leader in the way it trains people.

That's good. About the motorbike, is it very expensive to insure?

People often ask that, but in fact it's much cheaper to insure than a car. Financially, it's the optimal solution to commuting, if you're prepared to accept the risk of riding it. But as I say, not everyone wants to make that trade-off, which I can understand.

I see. Now we'll discuss things people use in their daily life.

Part 3

What machine or device do you think is most important in everyday life?

Well, people could debate that question all day. I think I'd instinctively say the phone, because it serves so many different purposes and has so many functions in people's lives. That means not just keeping in touch with people, but using maps, doing banking and shopping, and using apps to organise your whole life. But equally, what about machines like cars and trucks? Without them, daily life would come to a standstill in minutes, and even basic services like our food supply would break down. Then there are all the other machines we need to have, whether for cooking or cleaning or other tasks that have to be done. So, I don't think we can identify one particular machine or gadget that's more important than others in that respect. They're all essential, just in different ways.

Okay, thanks. And how do you think daily life is different today compared to a hundred years ago?

Well, for one thing, we have all the devices we've just mentioned. To someone from the 1920s, they would be unbelievable. Not just in communications, but in heating and lighting, and of course in transportation. I read somewhere that in 1950, the total number of all the people in history who had ever been in an airplane was equivalent to a small rural town. But today, it's equivalent to the population of the USA and India combined. I think that was the figure. And that's maybe the central point, because not only is daily life easier and more comfortable than in the past, but these benefits are available to vastly more people around the world than they ever have been before. That's how I'd sum it up.

And what inventions for daily life are possibly coming in the future?

If we think of the next quarter century, for example, I think we'll see far more automation in people's homes. That means that windows and heating or ventilation systems will operate by themselves to maintain an ideal inside environment with the lowest use of energy. Another innovation I can imagine is the use of technology in clothing, which means clothes will keep people warm or cool by measuring the person's body readings and the conditions they're in, whether indoors or outside. Both of those are perfectly achievable in the next few years. On the other hand, one thing people have been promised for many years now is flying cars, but I don't believe they will ever be widely used. Not because of lack of technology, but because the vast majority of people aren't capable of flying a vehicle at speed in three dimensions, it's simply too demanding.

Why do you think that is?

Well, sorry to keep going on about motorbikes, but only about twenty percent of people are capable of riding a bike in two dimensions at speed. The other eighty percent just can't cope with the pace of the demands made on their brains, because humans weren't intended to do such a thing by nature. Flying a car through the air, with other flying cars around you too, would be unmanageable except for a tiny minority of people, the kind of people who become qualified pilots. For everyone else, it would be highly stressful and dangerous to even try. So I think flying cars will only ever be a specialist hobby, like being an amateur pilot at weekends.

I see what you mean. Thanks, that's the end of the test now.

***

Practice Test 13

Part 1

Let's discuss your work or studies at present
What plans or ambitions do you have?
Where will you work or study in future?
What qualifications or training will you need?

Part 2

Task card

Talk about an object or possession which is important to you
Say what this is and where you keep it
How and where you got it
Why it is important to you
And say what you do with this object or possession

Examiner's follow up questions

Do you know other people who have something similar?
What will you do with this in future?

Part 3

Let's discuss people's possessions
What are the most expensive items in a typical home?
What kind of purchases do people pay for in instalments?
How does the cost of living affect people?

***

Practice Test 13: Candidate's Page ✂

The examiner should cut this page from the book and give it to the candidate in Part 2, but not before

Part 2 Task card

Talk about an object or possession which is important to you
Say what this is and where you keep it
How and where you got it
Why it is important to you
And say what you do with this object or possession

Space for Candidate to Make Notes in One-Minute Preparation Time

Band 9 Example of Practice Test 13

Part 1

Let's start by talking about your work or studies. Are you working currently?

Well, I am, but it's just a part time job because I'm finishing some exams at the moment. My studies are the big focus for me right now, so they get all my attention.

And what are you studying?

I'm trying to qualify to be a speech therapist, which is the job where you help people to change the way they speak in some way, usually because of problems in the way they produce words. It's something I've always wanted to do, and I'm close to achieving it now.

Great. Why is that your ambition?

Well, my brother had a speech problem when he was a small child, and a speech therapist helped him overcome it through therapy. That made a huge difference to his life and wellbeing, and it made a big impression on me, so that's where it started.

Thanks. Are the exams hard?

I wouldn't say they're difficult, but the sheer amount of material you have to learn is enormous. That's why I'm devoting so much time to preparing for them, because, if you fail, you're not allowed to take them again.

I see. Where will you work when you do pass?

Thanks for your confidence in my abilities. I could work for a health centre in the capital, but I've never really wanted to live there because it's so chaotic. Another option is to take a position in Singapore, because they recognise our national qualifications, and from what I've heard it's an amazing place to live. I think that's the best choice, in fact.

So you're studying full time now, apart from your job?

Yes, I'm at college for thirty hours a week, which includes work placements at speech therapy clinics. My job is only eight hours a week, and it's fun anyway, so I don't mind doing it.

What's your job?

I work at a clothes store in the mall on the central boulevard here. I like clothes and fashion, and to be honest most of the people who come into the store are friends of mine. That means it's completely stress-free, unlike a lot of retail jobs these days.

Yes. You mentioned moving to Singapore, do you know anyone there?

I have a contact at one of the main hospitals, a doctor I met at a conference who said they would welcome an application from me if I qualify. And I know someone who moved there last year, who says he's very pleased with the move and he plans to stay. So, I could start to find my way around a bit.

Will you need to take further qualifications?

Yes, if I'm going to progress with speech therapy as a career, I'll need to specialise in an area and take a further qualification in that. So, for example, I might specialise in treating children, or people who have injuries that affect their speech. Either of those fields would be fascinating to research further.

Good. Now we'll start part two, you can prepare for a minute, then please speak for one to two minutes.

Part 2

Task card

Talk about an object or possession which is important to you
Say what this is and where you keep it
How and where you got it
Why it is important to you
And say what you do with this object or possession

Candidate's notes during one minute preparation

Telescope, how it works, keep it on balcony
Dad bought it, month's salary, one of the family
Important influence, childhood memories, my brother
See planets, take photos, put in frames for pictures

Can you speak now, please.

Yes, I'm going to talk about something important to me, not my personal possession because it belongs to my whole family and not just to me. This is a telescope which is quite a large piece of equipment, suitable for looking at the moon in detail or at planets or constellations in the sky at night. When I say it's large, I mean it's about a metre long, and it rests on a tripod stand with adjustable controls that allow you to change its angle and point it where you want. Then the telescope itself has a fine adjustment mechanism for focussing it precisely on the thing in the distance that you want to observe. To give you some idea of its power, if you focus it on the moon, you can see the craters and debris in amazing detail, almost as if you're in a plane flying over it. Or if you focus on Saturn, you can see the famous rings around the planet, which everyone has seen in photos but very few people ever actually see with the naked eye. We keep this telescope in my parents' apartment, in a room which has a balcony, so that we can move it out onto the balcony at night if we want to look at the sky. That's a delicate operation, of course, because a piece of equipment like that must always be handled very carefully.

Now, coming on to how we got this, my father bought it many years ago when he got his first job. He says he always wanted a proper telescope, because he'd always been interested in astronomy and space, so he spent his first month's salary on this one, and he's kept it ever since. So it's always been there ever since I can remember, obviously, and when we were small children my brother and I used to love looking at the planets and the moon through it. It's always been one of the family, you might even say, and it'd be difficult to imagine life without it standing there in the corner of the room.

I think that's why it's important to me, because it's one of those things which were a part of our childhood which we still have today, and we can still use it in the same way that we used to use it as children, if you see what I mean. It certainly had a big influence on my brother, because he's now doing astrophysics at university, and it was the telescope that started his interest in the whole subject.

In fact, we still use it quite regularly. A few times each month, we'll take it out onto the balcony and take a look at the moon or any planets which have changed position since the previous time. For example, a few weeks ago we had a good view of the planet Neptune at about eleven pm. The view isn't quite as clear as it used to be, because more buildings have been built around our apartment and so there's more electric light in the air, which gets in the way of the image you can see. Sometimes we even see satellites passing overhead; they're at a height of about two hundred kilometres, but we can see them clearly and we just have to wait until they're gone. But despite those problems, the telescope is good enough to allow us to take reasonable quality photos. We do that by using a special adaptor to put a mobile phone over the eyepiece of the telescope once the image we want is there. Then when we have the photo on a computer, we can work on it a bit to sharpen the colours and the resolution and so on, to get the best possible image that we can. These photos are very impressive sometimes, especially the ones of the moon or Saturn. In fact, we have a lot of these pictures in frames all over the apartment, and people always comment on them when they visit us. We're known locally as keen astronomers, because sometimes if we're in a store someone will say to us, 'Oh, you're the family with the telescope,' because everyone knows we have it. So, all in all, it's a fascinating thing to have, and very important to me because of its history and the role it still has in our family life.

(The candidate spoke for 2 minutes.)

Thanks. I suppose this is a traditional telescope, not a digital one?

Yes, it's what's called an optical scope, so it uses glass lenses in the traditional way. It may be surprising, but to get a digital one with the same power would be extremely expensive, because there's a limit to what a digital magnification can achieve unless it's very advanced.

I see. Is there a time of year that's best for using it?

Well, the night sky changes continuously during the year, as I'm sure you know, because the earth's orbit changes. That means there's always something new to see. But during spring there are sometimes meteor showers, which can be really dramatic if you see them when the moon is dark or below the horizon.

What do the meteors look like?

They're bright points that pass overhead quite rapidly. Last year we took a long video of them through the telescope, and you can see them appearing and then leaving over the horizon, it's very impressive.

Certainly. Well, let's move on to part three now, and we'll talk about things people have in their homes.

Part 3

What are the most expensive items in a typical home in this country?

The most expensive item would probably be a car, but that's not really in the home itself, I suppose. So putting that aside, we would probably have the TV, if it's a big screen type, or maybe a computer if it's a high quality unit. We could add the refrigerator to the list, in fact, because they can be very expensive these days as well. On the other hand, if we include things like jewellery, many homes will have something like a ring or a necklace that might be worth more than any device or machine that they possess. For example, if you insure your home in this town, the insurers will pay for any electrical item that is stolen, but they put a limit on how much they'll cover if someone's jewellery is taken, which shows us how valuable that stuff can be. So, it depends if we include jewels in the list, otherwise it would be something electronic.

Thanks. What kind of purchases do people pay for in instalments?

'Instalment' means a monthly payment?

Yes.

Well, again, buying a car is often done by taking out a loan and paying monthly instalments until it's all paid for. That's because not many people have enough money available to pay for a car all at once, unless it's quite a cheap car. The same applies to a house or apartment, where you'd be a very lucky person to be able to buy one for cash in advance. Most people have to take out a mortgage over many years, sometimes up to twenty-five years, in fact. Those two things, a car and a home, are probably the most common things that people pay for over time.

How would you say people are affected by the cost of living?

Oh, in many ways. Everything is getting more and more expensive all the time, especially things which people simply have to buy, such as food, energy or gasoline. This means that people end up spending more and more of any income they have on basic necessities, with not much left over for enjoying themselves or following their hobbies or sports. That can have a big impact on people, because they have less potential for relaxation, and so they can get more stressed and anxious. Another impact is that people find it difficult to save up money for the future, so over the long term they may have a lower standard of living as they get older. There's another effect as well, which is that people ask for salary increases to try to keep pace with inflation, and that can lead to disputes and friction with their employers. So, overall, we have those three impacts, I think: less leisure spending, less savings, and higher demands for wage rises.

Thanks. That's the end of the test now.

***

Practice Test 14

Part 1

Let's discuss your future plans. What are your plans for study, work or travel?
Where will you go to achieve this?
How long will it take?
What plans do your friends have?

Part 2

Task card

Describe a meeting, interview or conversation you remember well
Say when and where this was
Who was involved
What you spoke about
And say what was the outcome or result

Examiner's follow up questions

What did you learn from this experience?
What advice would you give to someone in a similar situation?

Part 3

Let's discuss meetings. How do online meetings or interviews (Zoom etc) compare to meetings in person?
Can friends and family keep in touch online as in person?
What are the advantages/disadvantages of working from home?
How will meetings or interviews change in future?

***

Practice Test 14: Candidate's Page ✄

The examiner should cut this page from the book and give it to the candidate in Part 2, but not before

Part 2 Task card

Describe a meeting, interview or conversation you remember well
Say when and where this was
Who was involved
What you spoke about
And say what was the outcome or result

Space for Candidate to Make Notes in One-Minute Preparation Time

Band 9 Example of Practice Test 14

Part 1

Let's start with your plans for the future. What are your plans for work, study or personal interests?

Talking about personal interests, I'm planning a trip to Australia at the moment. The idea is to go with three friends from work, which means we need to book the flights and accommodation in advance. That's something I'm looking into now, in fact.

When do you plan to go?

It will be in November, hopefully, which, from what I've heard, is when the weather there isn't too hot. It's their summer, obviously, and apparently in January it can be incredibly hot.

Whereabouts will you go in Australia?

This is where the planning is a bit complex. We'll fly to Sydney and have a few days there, then take internal flights to two other cities, which are Cairns and Darwin. They're in the north of the country, and it's a long journey, too far to drive.

Have you been before?

I haven't, although I've always wanted to. For example, I'd love to see Sydney opera house in person, not just on videos. But one of my friends has been before, which means she knows how to get around and make the most of the time we have there.

Do you all speak English?

Yes, to a similar level. I find the Australian accent a bit hard to understand sometimes, but I think we'll manage. It's not as bad as a really strong American accent, which I really struggle with.

You mentioned they're work friends, what job do you do?

I work for a company that does catering services to large events. That means we cater the complete food service for large weddings, for instance, and for things like sports events and other big gatherings.

What's your role there, is it the food itself?

Oh no, I'm terrible at cooking, unfortunately. I'm customer-facing, so I sell the packages to potential clients, and I coordinate the service itself depending on the price. It's quite pressurised, but I enjoy that.

How is it pressurised?

Well, I have a target of selling a certain number of packages across the year, so I have to hit that. So every time a possible new client gets in contact, I have to do everything possible to convert them to a paying customer. That's what I mean by pressure, but it's not a great problem at all.

What sort of plans do you have for your work?

At some point, I'd like to start my own business. That would probably be in recruitment, which means finding candidates for jobs available at large companies. It's a very competitive area, but the rewards can be very high.

Thanks. We'll come on to part two now. Here's your task card, please prepare and then speak for one to two minutes.

Part 2

Task card

Describe a meeting, interview or conversation you remember well
Say when and where this was
Who was involved
What you spoke about
And say what was the outcome or result

Candidate's notes during one minute preparation

Job interview, July 2 years ago, radio station, advertising role
Director, 2 execs, surprising coincidence, atmosphere
Interview, my CV, strange situation, 2 levels of thoughts
Had job offer, turned it down, right decision today

Okay, please start speaking now.

Well, I'm going to talk about a job interview I had, not for my current job at the catering company, but another application I made around the same time. This all took place two years ago, in July; in fact, it was just before the flooding that we had at that time. I applied to work at a radio station. Now, this radio station is well known locally, and it was a very desirable job to have, because everyone knows the station for the quality of its programmes. The job itself involved selling radio advertising to potential customers in the broadcasting area, which was this city and all the surrounding towns. I applied online, and they emailed me, inviting me for a meeting with the head of advertising. So I went to the radio station offices at the agreed time, which was early afternoon, and I was shown to the office of the advertising director.

When I stepped into the office, it wasn't just the director in there, but a panel of three people including her, meaning the director, and two others. The others turned out to be advertising sales executives who were currently with the station. This was all a bit unsettling for me, because for one thing I wasn't expecting to be confronted with three people in the interview, there had been no mention of that at all. And that wasn't the only odd thing, because I thought straight away that I recognised one of the advertising execs from somewhere, and then, when he told me his name, I realised who he was. He was a boy who attended my school when we were children, and I remembered him because we didn't get along with each other at all. In fact, it's no exaggeration to say that we disliked each other intensely. As we were sitting there starting the interview, I could see he was looking at me and I'm sure he remembered who I was as well.

As you can imagine, it was a very strange interview, because all the time I was responding to their questions and talking about my CV, I was recalling in my mind all the times that I'd had disagreements and fights with this person when we were just kids. I think it's an experience that people sometimes have, when they've largely forgotten about a person, but then seeing them again suddenly brings back memories and it's all very vivid in the mind again. So this interview was kind of taking place on two levels, because on one level we were talking about my career and previous jobs, and I was trying to portray myself as very successful and put myself in the best possible light, as one does. But on another level, I was remembering my schooldays and thinking how annoying and unpleasant this other guy was at the time. Then, at one point, the advertising director said to me, 'The job you're applying for is a post reporting to him,' and she pointed at my old childhood enemy. That meant this person was going to be my boss at the radio station if I got the job. Well, that put me in a difficult position, because I certainly didn't want the job, but equally I didn't want to walk out of the interview, because that would be very unprofessional. Who knows when I might meet that advertising director again? You should always stay on good terms with anyone you meet professionally, that's one of my principles. Anyway, the interview came to a close, and we all said goodbye. Normally, when you leave an interview, you're thinking, 'I hope I get this job,' but in this case I was saying to myself, 'I'd hate to do this job.'

One final strange thing happened, which was that they offered me the job the next day by email. That was a complete surprise, because of the person involved, and I couldn't understand why my old enemy wanted me to work with him. In fact, I found it a bit suspicious, and I certainly didn't want to accept it. Fortunately, I had an offer from the catering firm at the same time, so I replied to the radio station very politely, saying that their job wasn't right for me and wishing them all the best with finding a candidate. I'm sure that was the right decision to make, in retrospect, because I'm very happy at the catering firm, and it's going very well in terms of the work itself. So it was a strange experience, but I got away with nothing worse than a wasted afternoon. That's not a bad outcome, really.

(The candidate spoke for 1 minute 45 seconds.)

Thanks for that. You're sure this was the same person, from school?

Yes, after the interview I looked him up online, and it was definitely him. I suppose it's possible that he had a huge change of personality since school, but somehow I doubt it.

I see. What advice would you give people generally about job interviews?

For one thing, people should prepare carefully by finding out about the employer and the role itself. And another point is just to be yourself in the interview, don't try to put on an act or pretend to be someone else.

Okay, thanks, and now we'll come onto part three.

Part 3

Let's discuss the ways people have meetings these days. What do you think of having meetings by Zoom, for example, compared to in person?

That's an interesting topic, actually. If we're talking about a professional context, then online meetings certainly have advantages, in terms of saving on travelling time and expense of course, and also being able to have more people in a meeting than maybe you could in person. The online option lets you invite people from other locations, maybe very distant locations, who wouldn't be able to attend in person. There's also the fact that you have a permanent record of exactly what was said, if you record it and do a speech-to-text document. These are all big advantages. But on the other hand, there are weaknesses too. One is that a lot of people behave slightly differently online compared to in person, meaning that they're less likely to come up with ideas or suggestions. Another point is that it's harder to assess people's reaction to what you're saying, because all the little indicators like eye contact or body language are just a bit harder to see. Overall, I'd say that online meetings are very much a second best compared to face to face.

Thanks. What about friends and family, is it possible to keep in touch with them online in the same way as in person?

Well, that's a bit different, I think. With family and friends, you already know the person, so you know what interests them and what their mannerisms are. That means you'll find it easier to talk about things you have in common, and also it's easier to see their reaction to what you're saying, even if you're communicating online. Of course, it's not the same as seeing them in person, but I think there's less of a barrier than there can be in business meetings. We could even say that keeping in touch online helps a relationship, because you can communicate with them constantly through the day, and you can each see what the other person is doing. That makes it easier to exchange ideas or feelings, and that constant exchange can really help a relationship thrive, I think.

Thanks for that. What are the advantages or drawbacks of working from home?

That's a topical point, especially since the Covid situation. There are definitely some advantages to working from home, at least for the individual worker. There's a big saving on travel costs and time, and maybe without interruptions people can get more done in a working day. But on the other hand, not everyone has a home suitable for working from, and a lot of people actually enjoy the human contact of being in a workplace, even if they have to commute. Then if we consider the employer's angle, there's the danger that the workers aren't actually doing much all day, because how can it be monitored? All in all, I think the trend for working from home is slowly fading away, and rightly so in my opinion.

I see, thanks. Well, we've completed the whole test now.

***

Practice Test 15

Part 1

Let's discuss your home town. Can you describe it?
What are the buildings like?
Do you work or study in the town, or elsewhere?
Do you still live in the town?
What is your accommodation like?

Part 2

Task card

Describe a place you visit often
Say what and where this place is
How you started going there
Why you still go there
And say if you will continue to visit there in future

Examiner's follow up questions

Have you found any other places like this?
Has the place changed in the time you've known it?

Part 3

We'll discuss ways that people travel to make visits
Do people visit their families less today than the past?
How has tourist travel changed since the past?
Can you compare some different ways of travelling to work?

***

Practice Test 15: Candidate's Page ✂

The examiner should cut this page from the book and give it to the candidate in Part 2, but not before

Part 2 Task card

Describe a place you visit often
Say what and where this place is
How you started going there
Why you still go there
And say if you will continue to visit there in future

Space for Candidate to Make Notes in One-Minute Preparation Time

Band 9 Example of Practice Test 15

Part 1

Let's begin by talking about your home town or city. Can you describe it?

Well, it's more of a village, frankly, because I don't think there are enough people to call it a town. It's a small community in the countryside, just inland from the main port. That means it benefits economically from being near the docks, but it's still quite traditional.

How does it benefit economically?

I mean that, in addition to the traditional industries, which are farming and cutting timber, people can also opt to go and work at the port as well. We're very lucky in that sense, because it means there's almost no unemployment at all.

Thanks. What are the buildings like in the village?

It's very mixed, because there are some old nineteenth century houses, which today are often small hotels, and also a couple of apartment blocks, which date from the mid twentieth century, I suppose. On top of that, there are various barns and timber warehouses dotted around, as you'd expect.

I see. Do you yourself work traditionally or at the port?

I've done both, actually. I worked on farm part-time when I was at high school, until I graduated, and then I started working at the port as a customs officer. Both are very enjoyable, but I prefer the customs work.

What does that involve?

We keep a database of all the goods coming into the port, including the place of origin, the volumes, and the value. That's used by the government to put taxes on some of the products, but not all. We also have a security role, which means making sure that nothing dangerous or illegal comes in without being detected.

Why do you enjoy it?

It's a great team of people to work with. I'm the youngest one, as you can probably guess, but the training has been excellent and I can definitely see a future with customs. That's why I'm taking this IELTS test, in fact.

Have they asked you to take the test?

Well, they've offered me training in what's called investigative accounting, which means analysing financial records for evidence of crimes. As part of that, I could do a year studying at a British university on a specialised accounting course, because those courses have a good reputation.

Which university would it be?

Maybe Southampton, because our customs office has sent people there before, to do various programmes. I don't know anything about Southampton, but I'm sure it will be fine as a place to live.

I'm sure. And, in the village, do you live with your family or independently?

I live with my parents at the moment, and I commute daily down to the port. It takes about half an hour, so that's not too bad, and I have the advantages of living at home still. I'm planning to move out, but it depends on what happens with the course I mentioned.

Sure. Where would you move to?

If I don't go abroad, I'll probably move to the port, because the customs office has some apartments which they rent out to the staff. They're nothing special, quite frankly, but it means I could walk to work in ten minutes.

What sort of home do your parents have?

It's an apartment in one of the blocks in the village. We're lucky, because it faces out over the open countryside, not the road, so the view is brilliant. We can see all the way to the mountains in the distance, and that's quite a long way.

Do you ever go to the mountains?

Yes, I've been skiing there a few times. I'm not a great skier, though, for some reason. Some people spend every weekend there in winter, but it doesn't appeal to me that much.

Okay, thanks. Let's do Part 2 now, and here's your topic.

Part 2

Task card

Describe a place you visit often
Say what and where this place is
How you started going there
Why you still go there
And say if you will continue to visit there in future

Candidate's notes during one minute preparation

Village Grill – position, appearance, tables, grill

As children, families, '2ⁿᵈ home/garden,' teenagers still went there
Handy to still go there, way home from work, old friends still
around
May continue going – depends on ownership – motel?!

Can you start speaking now, please.

Yes, I'll talk about a restaurant which is near my village, on the road between my home and the port itself. It's only about two kilometres from my house, and it's set back from the road in an area of fields. There's a big parking area at the front, so you can always find a place to park your car or bike, and at the back there's a play area for children, with swings and slides and so on. Then, positioned all around it, there are outside tables and benches with sun shades over the top. That's important, because it can get very hot in summer away from the coast, as you know. Inside, there's a lot more seating, and a huge open grill where the cooks make the food. This restaurant is called 'The Village Grill' if you translate it to English, and it's famous in the area for offering excellent quality food at very good value prices. It's not sophisticated food, like fine dining, but it's authentic national cooking, and it's very tasty.

Well, I started going to The Village Grill as a child, along with almost all the other children from the village where I live. Especially in summer, all the families would go along there at some point over the weekend, or maybe in the week at times. The play area for children that I mentioned was great fun for us to play around on, and we would get an ice cream or something while the parents had a coffee or something to eat. Especially for those families, like us, who didn't have a garden, it was like our second home at times. Then, as we got older, many of us got into the habit of going there without our parents, around the time when got our first motor scooters or cars. It was a very convenient place for us all to meet up and sit around talking. We would make a Coca Cola and some French fries last for ages, just so that we could sit there chatting.

Obviously, we were all very well behaved, so the staff had no problem with us being there.

As time went by, we'd go there a bit less, because we all became more interested in going into the city for our free time, rather than the same old place we'd grown up in. But recently, I've started going there more and more, especially on the way home from work sometimes, or on weekend afternoons. There's a group of us who all grew up together, and we're the ones still left, you might say, because a lot of our peer group have moved away by now. These days we enjoy sitting there, but talking about slightly more adult things, such as who's getting promoted at work or who's going to get their own accommodation, and so on. And, of course, it's still a very inexpensive place to go, so that suits us as well. These days we don't have to make a single soda drink last all night, though, which the staff are probably pleased about as well.

Thinking of the future, I think it's pretty likely that I'll keep on going to the restaurant, assuming that I still live in the village. I mean, if I end up living in the city, I don't think I'd make the trip out there just to go to the Grill. I might stop off there if I go back to visit my parents, or maybe take my parents there for lunch or something like that. Another aspect that might change things is whether the place stays under the same ownership, because people say the current owner is thinking of selling up and retiring after all these years. There's a rumour that a big company might buy the place and turn it into a motel for tourists, because visitors go to the area more and more for hiking and skiing. That would be a real shame, because I'm sure it would change the character of the place, and maybe change the wonderful food as well. I don't think I'd go back there if it was taken over like that, because it wouldn't have the same atmosphere at all. So, it depends on my circumstances in the future, and also what happens to the place itself.

(The candidate spoke for 1 minute 55 seconds.)

Thanks for speaking. What's a typical meal there?

Oh, they're famous for their grilled meat and cheese, which all comes from local farms, and it's very good quality indeed. Everything is made on the grill, you see, which is how people in the area used to cook years ago in their farmhouses.

Has the restaurant changed much since you were a child?

It hasn't changed much at all, to be honest. It's all rather frozen in time, I think the phrase is like a time capsule. I think if they updated it, some of the charm would be lost. By the way, most of the staff are the same as when I was a kid, so they started out as teenagers and now they're middle-aged. The owner is getting quite elderly too.

Have you found similar places in other areas?

Actually, no, I haven't. I often see little restaurants in other towns and cities, but I don't think there's anything quite like our restaurant, and the way in serves as a kind of second home for the community around it.

Thanks. Now for Part 3 of the test, we'll be discussing the way people travel to visit places and people.

Part 3

Do you think people visit their families less today than in the past?

I'd say that it's hard to generalise. On the one hand, we might say that because people are so busy today, they see their families less, especially if they end up in different areas. It's not unusual for an adult to only see their sibling once or twice a year, for example, if they live at a distance. But, on the other hand, that was probably true in the past as well, as people moved around for work or marriage. Also, the fact it's so quick to travel to visit your relatives means that it's easier than in the past, when it was so slow that it maybe wasn't worth making the effort. All in all, I'm not really sure it's correct to say we visit our families less today. I think it's probably about the same, really.

Thanks. What are the advantages of some different possible ways to get to work?

Different ways of commuting? Well, one popular way is by train, which has the advantages of being quite comfortable and not being at risk of traffic jams. It's also possible to read, or watch videos or work while you're on the train, which is important to a lot of people. It tends to be quite hot and overcrowded, though. Another very common means of transport is the private car, which has the benefit of taking you directly to the destination. It also insulates you from the weather outside, and from other people, which must be one reason for its popularity. There's a third method of getting to work, which is cycling. That's especially good if there are dedicated cycle lanes on the roads you use, and if the weather is suitable, and assuming, of course, that a person is physically able to cycle. I think those three are the main methods of commuting.

Okay. How has tourist travel changed since the early twentieth century?

The changes have been enormous, I think. Firstly, it's quite common now for people to visit other countries for vacations, which a hundred years ago was rare. Secondly, methods of transport are much faster, safer and more comfortable than in the past. For example, passenger planes today have levels of comfort that were unimaginable in the past, even in basic economy class. Another example is the way you could decide to fly to somewhere half way around the world, and the trip would take maybe ten or twelve hours. In the old days, with ships and trains, it would have been very complicated and would probably take weeks. So, availability, comfort and speed are the big changes for tourists, I would say.

Thanks for that. We've finished the test now.

***

Practice Test 16

Part 1

Let's talk about your family and friends.
What do your friends do in their spare time?
Where do you meet your friends? How do you stay in touch?
Do you live with your family?
What do your family do with their free time?

Part 2

Task card

Describe a famous or historic place you have seen personally
Say where and what this place is
When and how you went there
What you saw and did there
And say why you remember this place

Examiner's follow up questions

Would you recommend a trip to this place?
What similar places have you seen?

Part 3

We'll discuss historic places and sites
Are people becoming less interested in these sites?
Why are some historic places so famous?
What can governments do to protect historic sites?
What can individuals do?

***

Practice Test 16: Candidate's Page ✂

The examiner should cut this page from the book and give it to the candidate in Part 2, but not before

Part 2 Task card

Describe a famous or historic place you have seen personally
Say where and what this place is
When and how you went there
What you saw and did there
And say why you remember this place

Space for Candidate to Make Notes in One-Minute Preparation Time

Band 9 Example of Practice Test 16

Part 1

We'll start by talking about your friends. What do you do together in your spare time?

Most of my friends here are at the language school I go to. Between studying English and the jobs they have, they don't really have much free time, and neither do I in fact. But when we can, we like to go ice skating at the rink in town, or meeting for coffee and pastries at a coffee shop in the mall.

Why do you like ice skating?

Well, one of my friends was a champion ice skater in her home country, and she even won some prizes, I think. She's taught us how to skate really well, although we're not at her level just yet. That means we can all skate together for an hour or two, and we can chat and joke while we're skating in a group.

I see. How long have you been here at the language school?

Let me think . . . eight months now, since last September. But some of my friends have been at the school for years, literally, studying and working quite happily. None of us has any plans to go home, to be honest.

Okay. How do you stay in touch with your friends from your home country?

Oh, we're in touch all the time on messaging and chat. I haven't seen my best friend from home since I got here, but we message six or seven times a day, so we always know what the other person is doing.

When you're back home, do you live with your family?

Yes, over there I live with my parents and two sisters. My sisters are twins and they're much younger than me, so they're still at school. I speak to them every day, not just messaging but actually speaking to them, which is lovely and stops me getting homesick.

What do your family do with their free time?

Well, the twins are really keen soccer players, and they spend a lot of time at practice sessions and then playing matches all over the place. That means my parents tend to drive them around all the time, like taxi drivers. My mum's car has a sticker in the back which says 'Mother's taxi' as a joke.

What about here, who do you live with?

I rent an apartment with two other people from my country. We didn't really know each other when we moved in, but now we're good friends and we get along very well. It's a bit of a risk sharing a place without knowing the others first, but it's worked out very well.

Thanks. What sort of apartment is it?

It's on the top floor of a house near the river, so it's nice and quiet. The rooms we have are reasonably big and comfortable, so we're happy there. The only problem is that there's no elevator, so we have to walk up three flights of stairs, which if you've got all your groceries in bags is a bit much.

Okay, thanks, that's Part 1 finished. In Part 2, here's your card to speak about for one to two minutes. You can prepare first for a minute.

Part 2

Task card

Describe a famous or historic place you have seen personally
Say where and what this place is
When and how you went there
What you saw and did there
And say why you remember this place

Candidate's notes during one minute preparation

Buckingham Palace, position, fountain, size, guard uniforms, hats
Went on train, February – lunch
Impressive, crowds outside, cars, guards, went on tour, rooms, stairs
Contrast guards with police, friendly police/unfriendly guards

Okay, please begin now.

Okay, I'm going to talk about a very historic place I've been to, which is Buckingham Palace in London. This is the home of the King of the United Kingdom, or maybe I should say it's one of his homes, because I think there are others he uses, such as Windsor Castle. It's located right in the heart of London, which itself is only about an hour from here on the train. It's across the river from the Houses of Parliament, and it's positioned in an open area which has a huge fountain in the middle of it. It's the largest fountain I've ever seen, in fact, with enormous statues of what I think are mermaids on it. The building itself is enormous as well, and it takes up an area the size of a city block, hundreds of meters on each side. It's surrounded by tall metal railings, and inside you can see guards who look like something from two hundred years ago, with ceremonial swords and very large hats. That's the whole idea, I suppose, to show that the institution hasn't changed for centuries, and to say it will never change. By the way, I think the hats are made from bear skins, which seems rather cruel to me.

221

Anyway, I went to see Buckingham Palace in February this year. It was a fairly bright day, and at least it wasn't raining. I went with two friends on the train, and we got there in time for lunch. One thing I've learned is never to buy food from the café on a British train, it's absolutely terrible and it costs a fortune. So, by the time we got there, we were pretty hungry, and we had lunch at a very nice Greek café near the station. After that we were ready to do some sightseeing, so we took the underground, the tube as they call it, to near the palace.

When we got there, it was a very impressive sight, probably even more striking than we expected from seeing pictures and videos. I remember there was some mist in the air, but the sun was coming out as well, so it looked almost like a movie for a few minutes until the mist went away. There was a big crowd of people moving around the area in front of the palace by the railings, and people were taking photos and posing for selfies and so on, as you'd expect. Now and then, a big official limousine would pull up to the gates, and the guards would let it go through into the central area, and the car would disappear through an arch into the inside of the building. It was noticeable that the guards on the inside were in the old ceremonial uniform, but on the outside there were lots of modern guards, I mean police with guns and radios just like the police anywhere else. Well, after a while taking photos, we joined a queue and went into the palace to see the inside, because we'd booked tickets for the inside tour which they offer. The tour was very interesting, because we saw a lot of the huge meeting rooms in the palace, which they call state rooms, which were amazing to see. They were all lined with huge paintings on the walls, and enormous glass lamps on the ceilings which I think are called chandeliers. We saw some of the staircases too, which are incredibly wide, and we saw the way they connect various parts of the palace together. We also got close to some of the ceremonial guards that are positioned around the building at certain points, and we were impressed at how they stayed completely calm and still, even with lots of people like us swarming around and taking pictures of them.

Actually, that's one reason why I remember the visit so well, because there was a big contrast between the old-fashioned guards inside and the modern armed police outside. The ones inside were obviously under orders not to interact with the public, because they wouldn't respond to anything that anyone said, even if someone tried to speak to them directly, which we weren't supposed to do. But the police outside were very friendly, and they would say hello to people in the queue and exchange a few words with the tourists. They were much friendlier than police I've seen in other countries. I mentioned this to a British person I know, and he said that in fact the London police behave like that as a way of assessing the crowd, to see if anyone behaves strangely and might be suspicious or dangerous before they go inside the palace. So, all the time these police were smiling and saying hello, they were actually checking people out and making decisions about them, apparently. Having said all that, I'm glad I had a day there, because it was well worth making the trip.

(The candidate spoke for 1 minute 45 seconds.)

Thanks for that. Have you seen any similar places in other countries?

Well, I've seen the presidential palace in my country, which is a similar size but more modern. But you're not allowed to see the inside of it, for security reasons, so it's not really a day trip like Buckingham Palace. And the police outside are definitely less friendly, to be honest.

I see. What else have you seen in London?

Oh, all the usual tourist sights. My favourite one was the London Eye, which is a big wheel that lifts you up so you can see all of

London from the air. I've been on that twice, in fact, because I liked it so much.

Thanks. Now let's go onto Part 3, and we'll discuss historic places and traditions.

Part 3

What can governments do to protect historic sites and buildings?

Well, that's an important job for any government to carry out. Maybe the main thing they can do is to provide funding so that the buildings themselves can be properly protected and maintained. Of course, that's easy to say, but the cost of all the maintenance is very high, so inevitably the government will have to prioritise some sites over others. Another step the state can take is to educate young people about why these places are so important, so that each generation understands and recognises their value. Hopefully, schools will do that as part of history and culture lessons. I think that by doing those two things, funding and education, the government will be doing most of the job.

Thanks. What can individuals do to help?

Individuals can help, first of all, by actually going to visit the places and seeing them for themselves. If we're going to all the trouble and expense of maintaining an old palace or statue or something, we want people to actually visit and see all the good work. Another helpful thing is to treat these sites with respect, meaning not dropping litter or vandalising them, especially if they're in a city centre. People can also spread the message about how interesting these places are, for example by leaving online reviews or through social media, so that everyone knows they're important and worth seeing. All of that would certainly help.

Thanks. Do you think people are becoming less interested in historic places?

In some ways, that might be true. For example, I think some young people would be less interested in a day trip to a historic place if there are other attractions available, such as sports or a social activity. But on the other hand, I think as those young people get older and maybe have families, they'll start to develop more of an interest in the past, and hopefully pass that on to their children. So I think it depends on people's age, but I also think that each generation discovers an increased interest in these things as time goes by. So it's kind of a cycle, we could say.

I see, thanks. We've finished the test now.

***

Practice Test 17

Part 1

Let's talk about your studies, work or career
What work do you do?
Did you consider other types of careers before this?
What would you like to do in future?
Will you need further qualifications?

Part 2

Task card

Talk about a place in nature that has impressed you
Say where and what this is
When you saw it
Describe what it was like
And say why this place in nature impressed you

Examiner's follow up questions

Do you think this place has changed since you saw it?
Have you seen any similar places?

Part 3

We'll discuss how to protect the natural world
What are the main threats to the natural world today?
How can these risks be reduced?
Will electric vehicles make a difference?
How will our attitudes to nature change in future?

***

Practice Test 17: Candidate's Page ✂

The examiner should cut this page from the book and give it to the candidate in Part 2, but not before

Part 2 Task card

Talk about a place in nature that has impressed you
Say where and what this is
When you saw it
Describe what it was like
And say why this place in nature impressed you

Space for Candidate to Make Notes in One-Minute Preparation Time

Band 9 Example of Practice Test 17

Part 1

Let's talk about your career, if possible. Do you work?

Well, I'm very much at the start of my career right now. I have an online influencing business, which means companies pay me to tell my followers about their products or services. I run this mainly off a YouTube channel and lots of other media.

That's interesting. How did you get involved with that?

I had a normal job, in a restaurant in fact, as a junior manager. It was very stressful and really quite exhausting, but I've always loved food and the restaurant business. So I began doing reviews of restaurants, judging them on different criteria, and it took off from there.

The companies who pay you are restaurants, then?

They're restaurants, hotels, food companies and that sort of profile. My followers like to be the first people to learn about a new venue, or a new dish or ingredient, so companies planning something new will hopefully come to me to publicise it.

Did you consider other careers before this?

Yes, before working as a restaurant manager I actually studied to be an architect briefly. That was my original long-term plan. But it didn't suit me at all, and neither did the manager role, whereas what I'm doing right now is absolutely ideal for me.

Why does it suit you so well?

I suppose because I'm completely independent and I can do everything just the way I want to, without anyone else interfering. That doesn't mean it's easy, though. I'll typically work ten or twelve hours a day across all my different platforms or projects, and that's six days a week.

Do you need any training, for the technology involved?

I do have people who advise me on how to get the most out of the different platforms, but it's very informal. A lot of this work consists of trying things out for yourself and seeing what works and what doesn't. That suits me as well, the fact that it's very experimental.

Thanks. And how do you see this developing in future?

I'm hoping it will get bigger and bigger, until I reach the point where I can pick and choose which sponsors to have. At that point, I can start to maybe work a bit less intensively, allowing me to research new developments in food a bit more. I'd like to be someone who goes around the world, finding new things about food to bring to my followers.

When do you think that will happen?

I'm not sure, but hopefully in the next three years, roughly speaking. It's certainly been a strong start for me, but the challenge is to take it to the next level, rather than keep doing the same thing continuously. My followers want new things and more exciting things all the time.

Thanks, and we'll go on to Part 2 now. Here's your topic, please prepare and then speak for up to two minutes.

Part 2

Task card

230

Talk about a place in nature that has impressed you
Say where and what this is
When you saw it
Describe what you did there and what it was like
And say why this place in nature impressed you

Candidate's notes during one minute preparation

Burning Water (translation) location, position in ravine, rapids
Hiking trip at 20, camping, not white water type
Walking up to it, speed of water, down to river, across boulders,
describe the water
Exciting, risk of falling, the fear, friend's comment after

Well, can you please speak now for one to two minutes.

I'm going to speak about a place I once saw, which has a name that in English means 'Burning Water.' This is located in the south of my country, in an area which is well known for lakes and rivers. There's one river in particular which is very wide and deep, and it flows quickly because it's close to meeting the sea at that point. There's one particular place where the river gets much narrower, because it has to go in a ravine between two very high walls of rock. I think that over millions of years the river has worked its way through the rock, and it's created a channel of water that's only about thirty metres wide. What's remarkable is that when the river comes out of the ravine or channel, it falls over a long slope of rocks and boulders, which most people call rapids. This makes the water very noisy and white, and this is why the indigenous people called it 'Burning Water' when they found it.

Well, I saw this phenomenon just once, which was on a hiking trip through that part of the country five years ago, when I was twenty. I was with a group of friends from college at that time. We had been hiking around the lakes which are scattered around the area,

231

some of them very beautiful, and we were sleeping in tents at campsites along the way. We had all heard of 'Burning Water' and seen pictures of it, so it was one of the places we definitely wanted to see up close along the way. You might think that the type of water I described would be ideal for what's called white water rafting, where you go down some rapids in an inflatable boat very fast, and you need to paddle to stop the boat turning over. But 'Burning Water' isn't suitable for that, because the rocks are piled up in such a way that a boat wouldn't be able to get through. This is what makes the water so fierce and so full of energy, because it's being forced through a series of very narrow openings between boulders that would stop a boat. But one thing you can do is walk across the rapids, from one bank to another, by climbing from one boulder to another very carefully. That's what we planned to do.

Well, we approached the place by walking along the top of the side of the ravine. This was an amazing sight, because we could look down and see the water in the channel maybe fifty metres below us. The water appeared to be very dark and still, but it was moving at high speed towards its exit point. One of us dropped a piece of tree branch into the water, and it was carried forward incredibly quickly in that direction. It took us a long time to walk along the channel, and we could hear the rapids at the other end getting louder. When we finally got there, we could see the whole area of rapids in front of us, with the water surging very fast through the rocks.

We climbed down from the top of the channel down to the river level, and we found the line of boulders that you can walk across. This meant that we had to climb from one rock to the next, with the river making an incredible noise underneath us. It was such an exciting and fascinating thing to do, because of course if you did slip off the rock, you'd fall into the water and find yourself in a terrible situation, probably a fatal situation. Sometimes it was easy to cross between the rocks, but in other places you had to jump and take the risk of falling. We stopped for a while about half way across to drink some water, and the view we had from there was amazing. The river was forcing itself under the boulders on one side, and shooting out in white water and spray on the other side. Sometimes we could see rainbows in the water spray, and then they would disappear as the light changed. In the end, we got to the other side and found a path that led away from the river and on to the next campsite we could use.

Well, as you can appreciate, this was an unforgettable experience in many ways. For one thing, to experience the huge energy of the river so close was amazing, and to see how the water behaved as it went through the obstructions. But on top of that, the experience of having to make yourself jump between the boulders, and overcome your instinctive fear of falling, was unlike anything I'd ever done before. As we were going away, one of my friends said, 'You know what? The river forced itself through the rocks, and so did we.' Well, we all stopped and looked at her, because it was a very true thing to say, and almost poetic, if you know what I mean.

(The candidate spoke for two minutes.)

Thanks for that, you've had two minutes. Have you ever seen anything similar?

No, not at all. I've seen other rapids, and I've been white water rafting, but 'Burning Water' is unique, as far as I know. It's also incredible that it's not very well known, even in my country. It's a well-kept secret, you could say.

Do you think it might change in future?

It's in a protected natural park area, so nobody can change it or build anything near it. Because of that, I think it has a good chance of staying unspoilt in the future, unless something happens to the river itself.

I see, thanks. Now we'll come on to Part 3, and we'll discuss how to protect the natural world generally, not only the place you described.

Part 3

What are the main threats to the natural world today?

The main threat is certainly climate change, because that could affect not just the world around us but also animal and human life if it gets out of hand. Another threat is pollution, especially from oil-based materials such as plastic, which is polluting to produce and also difficult to eliminate safely. There's a third threat, too, of course, which is uncontrolled human development spreading out into nature and taking over landscapes which should be left untouched. Those three threats are all connected together, and they all tend to make each other worse.

How can these risks be reduced?

I think it needs a very high level of international cooperation, to create programmes that try to solve all these problems in the same way all around the world. So that means a global programme on climate, another one on plastic, then on construction and so on. At the moment, every country is just following its own programmes, so, while the intentions may be good, there's no way of really planning or knowing what the outcome will be. Having a global framework would be the first step, before we start getting into all the fine details of individual programmes.

Thanks. Will electric vehicles make a difference?

Well, in some ways they should, because they don't produce emissions or pollutants when they're used. But it's not quite that simple, because their electric batteries are actually created using large amounts of metal, carbon and energy which cause a lot of emissions themselves. And, of course, the electricity to charge the batteries sometimes comes from fossil fuel power stations. So electric cars are a step forward, but they have complications that need to be fixed, especially in how they're produced.

How will our attitudes to nature change in future?

Let's hope people continue to be concerned and want to protect nature around us. That means, hopefully, that people will become better informed and educated about what's going on, and they'll have a greater enthusiasm for making reforms. We might also see more interest in what's called rewilding, which means allowing nature to expand back into previously developed areas such as cities or parks. That would allow natural habitats for animals to get larger and hopefully safer than at present. So, I think better education and more rewilding will be the two trends for the future.

I see, thanks. That concludes your test today.

***

Practice Test 18

Part 1

Let's talk about your home country
What are the main industries
What are the main holidays and festivals
What is the climate and weather like
What books and films are popular

Part 2

Task card

Speak about a meal or gathering you remember well
Say when and where this was
Who was present
What happened during the meal or gathering
And say why you remember it well

Examiner's follow up questions

Have you had a similar meal/gathering with those people since?
How often would you expect to do this?

Part 3

We'll discuss changes in food and eating habits
How have people's eating habits changed over time?
What risks are there in the modern diet in some countries?
Should advertisers target food products at children?
Should the government restrict sales of unhealthy foods?

***

Practice Test 18: Candidate's Page ✂

The examiner should cut this page from the book and give it to the candidate in Part 2, but not before

Part 2 Task card

Speak about a meal or gathering you remember well
Say when and where this was
Who was present
What happened during the meal or gathering
And say why you remember it well

Space for Candidate to Make Notes in One-Minute Preparation Time

Band 9 Example Of Practice Test 18

Part 1

Let's talk about your home country. What are the main industries?

The biggest industry is farming and processing what we grow. That means we grow a large amount of grain and vegetables, and we turn that into things like food oil, flour and cereal products. It's surprising, but a lot of food in the supermarkets here has ingredients from my country.

I see. How does your country export the products?

I think it must be mostly by ship, because we have a number of very large ports which connect to the big global markets. Road transport would be less suitable, because these are very bulky products and the road network isn't in great condition. Our government really should be doing something about that.

Okay. What do you think of the roads in this country?

The roads here? The infrastructure is excellent, but the maintenance of the roads themselves is quite poor. It's not as bad as in my country, but it's still quite disappointing to see.

Back to your country, what are the main festivals?

The main one is a three-day holiday in summer, which is partly a national independence celebration and partly an old religious holiday that people still observe. So all the businesses close, and there are a lot of processions and parades in the streets, which is interesting to watch.

What are these parades about?

Well, some are religious in nature, but others are demonstrations by political parties or trade unions. It's as if everyone is trying to have their voice heard above everyone else. There's also a major military parade, where the army show off their vehicles and the air force fly overhead, but that's just in the capital city.

Thanks. Are there any other holidays or festivals?

There are smaller holidays here and there on the calendar throughout the year. For example, in September, there's the national day of schools, when people take their children to school to begin the new academic year. Everyone gets a day off except the teachers and the children, unfortunately.

I see. And what's the climate like in your country?

It's very hot in summer and very cold in winter, with short transitions in between. That means that spring and autumn only last a few weeks until the heat or cold really set in. It's a shame, because the weather in those few weeks is very mild and pleasant.

What's it like in winter?

It's absolutely freezing, because the temperature can stay below zero for months on end. Fortunately, we're all adapted to it, and our houses and cars are prepared for all the ice and cold. Then, in summer, it's around thirty degrees for a long time and we all miss the snow, but I suppose that's inevitable.

Yes. What kind of films are popular?

What kind of movies . . . I think the Disney and Marvel movies are very popular with children and teenagers. The kids really love those superhero stories from the American studios, maybe because they're so full of action and technology. I have to say that adults don't go to the cinema very much, though, at least not these days.

And what about books, what's popular?

We're big readers of books, in fact. Book stores are always very busy, and people often have conversations about what they're reading. There's a science fiction book by one of our writers which has been incredibly popular over the last few years, and I think it's going to be a movie as well.

Why do you think that book has done so well?

Oh, because it's science fiction, but it's not full of robots and spaceships and all that stuff. It's set in the near future where a government is controlling people's minds by putting special messages through their phones. I'm trying to remember the right word . . . subliminal messages, which people don't realise they're hearing.

That sounds interesting.

It's an excellent book, I've read it myself. And although it's about the future, you can recognise our current government in the story as well. That's why people like it so much.

Thanks, and now we'll start Part 2. Here's your card, please prepare with some notes and then speak for one to two minutes.

Part 2

Task card

Speak about a meal or gathering you remember well
Say when and where this was
Who was present

What happened during the meal or gathering
And say why you remember it well

Candidate's notes during one minute preparation

Uni dinner, June, graduation, in the hall, boring reputation
Present: us, staff, waiting for speeches
Surprise: Ramon, song, our applause, more speeches
Memorable: Ramon contrast with speeches, unexpected, his
daughter

Can you please start now.

Okay, I'm going to speak about a meal I had last year, in June. This was in my home country, at the end of my university degree, because I'd just graduated from the university in my home city. You see, it's traditional at the end of a course for all the successful students to attend a ceremony where the certificates are awarded by the senior staff, which is usually held in the afternoon. The students' families attend this, and it's a very nice occasion. But then, in the evening, there's another tradition, which is that all the students gather together for a meal at the university. There aren't any family members present, just the students and staff, and it's generally held in a special hall on the campus. This hall is a very large building that can accommodate hundreds of people for an event, and it's used for things like orchestra performances, sports events and celebrations. For this meal, it was laid out with dozens of long tables with chairs either side, so that everyone could sit and eat. Now, to be honest, these graduation dinners have a reputation for being pretty dull. That's because all of the staff are there, and nobody wants to get too noisy and upset them, because they'll be the people writing a reference for you, for your first job or your next course. On top of that, there are traditionally a lot of speeches, which tend to be quite repetitive and boring. That's the reputations these dinners have always had, anyway.

On this particular evening, we all went into the hall at around seven pm, and we were greeted by the various tutors, lecturers, professors and university managers who were waiting to meet us. I was with a group of friends from my course, and we said hello to our lecturers and so on. This was pleasant enough, but the atmosphere was very flat, and nobody was really enjoying themselves. At one end of the hall there was a big stage equipped with microphones, and my friends and I said to each other, 'Oh, it's going to be a long night listening to speeches.' Well, we sat and ate the meal, which was very well-prepared. There was a series of traditional dishes, one in particular using fish which is often served at special occasions like this. We really appreciated the care that had gone into the food, in fact, and as the meal came to a close, we kind of settled back and made polite conversation with our tutors at the table. I was getting ready mentally for another hour or so of speeches.

At that point, something happened that was completely unexpected, in fact it was so surprising that we all stared at each other and said, 'What's going on?' This was because someone came onto the stage that we recognised, and we were all amazed to see it was someone called Ramon. Now, Ramon is very famous in my country, because he used to be a children's TV presenter a few years ago. He presented all the popular children's programmes and sang songs for them and that kind of thing. Everybody would recognise his face if they had kids, or if they grew up watching him on TV, as everyone in my age group did. It was very strange to see him on stage at the university, because he was so completely out of place. He was also older than in his TV days, of course, but still immediately recognisable. There was a real buzz of surprise going around the hall, as all the students turned to look at him. He stood at the microphone and said 'Are there any requests?' Someone shouted out, 'Rainbows On Monday!' Because that was the name of a children's song he used to sing on one of his programmes. Everybody knew that song, and he started to sing it in exactly the way he used to when we were all watching him on TV when we were ten years old. We were all absolutely staggered, and of course when he finished we broke into applause. People were cheering and banging the tables and shouting his name, yelling 'We love you, Ramon!' and so on. He bowed and waved to us, and acknowledged all the applause, and then he walked off stage and left. We never saw him again, it was just that one song. After that, the director of the university went on stage and said, 'Did you like the singing?' Of course, we all yelled, 'Yes!' But then we proceeded to have the hour of quite dull speeches that everyone was expecting. One speech after another from professors and managers, and they were all the more boring because of the incredible surprise of seeing Ramon in person.

We found out later that Ramon's daughter was going to study at the university the following year, and our director had invited him to make a speech. But Ramon didn't want to make a speech, he only wanted to sing his song, so he did. Apparently that's his personality, being quite a shy and private person, as a lot of entertainers are. That's why I remember this dinner so well, because of the astonishing surprise of seeing Ramon appear and then disappear, and also because of the contrast between his beautiful little performance and the very dull speeches which followed. A very strange contrast, but I'm sure everyone there will always remember the meal because of that.

(The candidate spoke for 1 minute 55 seconds.)

Thanks for speaking. Have you had any gatherings with all those people since then?

No, we haven't had a university reunion so far. If we ever do, I hope someone invites Ramon back, or maybe his daughter can persuade him to come along.

So Ramon is no longer on TV?

No, he stopped presenting a few years ago, for reasons I don't know, and people still wonder what on earth happened to him. I think he's just living a quiet life somewhere, so we were lucky to have seen him.

Sure. Well, lets move on to Part 3, and discuss food and eating habits.

Part 3

What risks are there in people's choice of food in some countries?

If we think of the heavily industrialised countries, there's a high level of risk in the amount of processed food that people eat. This kind of food contains a lot of artificial additives, and a lot of potentially unhealthy ingredients like sugar and salt. Another danger is certainly fast food such as takeaway burgers or chicken, which contains very high levels of fat and chemical preservatives. For example, a takeaway hamburger left on its own will take many months to decompose, because of all the preservatives in it. So I'd say processed food and fast food, those are the two big dangers in modern eating habits.

Thanks. Do you think advertisers should target food products at children?

It depends on what the product is, I think. If it's a healthy snack, or some sort of drink with natural ingredients, I think it's perfectly legitimate to advertise that to children. It might even persuade children to eat in a healthier way. On the other hand, if it's a very fattening or unhealthy product, something like a chocolate bar or a sugary drink, then it shouldn't be aimed at children at all. Kids often don't have the ability to reject things that are bad for them, so it would be completely unfair to advertise it to them.

I see. Should the government actively restrict the sales of unhealthy food items?

If we're talking about products which are extremely unhealthy, then I think there is a case for restricting or banning them, in the way that cigarette sales are restricted. The government would have to show that the products are dangerous to health, but the research should be able to prove that. But looking at it another way, if it's just a traditional product that people should be careful about consuming too much, such as chocolate or candy, I don't think it's feasible to ban things like that. They're too much a part of our daily lives. We can't really compare chocolate to cigarettes, because it's not as unhealthy as that, surely.

Thanks, that's the end of the test now.

***

Practice Test 19

Part 1

We'll discuss your spare time interests
What do you do for leisure
Where do you do this
What other people or equipment is involved
Why do you enjoy this
What are your plans for continuing this

Part 2

Task card

Describe a typical day in your life at present
Say what you do
Say where you go and who you meet
Describe what you do with these people
And say if you think this will change in future

Examiner's follow up questions

Is this typical day different from previous times in your life?
What do you enjoy about this typical day?

Part 3

We'll discuss how lifestyles are changing today
How are people's lifestyles changing today?
Are these changes positive? Why/why not?
What impact will AI have on lifestyles in the future?
Will standards of living be higher? Why/why not?

***

Practice Test 19: Candidate's Page ✂

The examiner should cut this page from the book and give it to the candidate in Part 2, but not before

Part 2 Task card

Describe a typical day in your life at present
Say what you do
Say where you go and who you meet
Describe what you do with these people
And say if you think this will change in future

Space for Candidate to Make Notes in One-Minute Preparation Time

Band 9 Example Of Practice Test 19

Part 1

Let's discuss your spare time interests. What do you do in your spare time?

My main interest is playing chess. I'm in the regional chess league, which means I play in competitions in this area, in the main cities. I'm hoping to be skilled enough to go up into the national league at some point.

Where do you play chess?

I play informally against other players I know online, because we trust each other not to use resources beyond our own minds. The competitions are played in venues like community centres or sports halls, because all the players have to be there in person and be seen not to have any support.

'Support' means getting advice from others?

Yes, it's an obvious danger. The players must be seen to have absolutely no input from other people. During the Covid pandemic, in fact, all chess competitions had to be suspended because people couldn't play in person. The tournaments couldn't be done online, because the international rules prohibit online play for exactly that reason.

Thanks. And why do you enjoy chess?

I enjoy the competitiveness of the tournaments, and the feeling of winning against someone who was trying their best to defeat me. Chess players are very competitive people, even if they seem rather quiet and reserved. I also like the fact that I learn something from every game I play. I mean that each game shows me a new move or a new way of responding to a move.

Is that how you increase your skill level?

Yes, the best players are able to store literally thousands of possible moves and counter moves in their minds, and they mentally review each possibility and its consequences as they're playing. There's that, and there's also the ability to imagine new sequences of moves that might win the game against that particular opponent.

How long have you been playing?

Ever since I can remember, really. My parents are both league players, and they started me off at a very young age. Chess often runs in families, because the parents are so dedicated to it and they want their children to play as well.

I see. What other interests do you have?

I like reading magazines and listening to podcasts in English, and watching English language movies. Sometimes I watch a movie and put the subtitles on in my own language, which really helps me learn new phrases and vocabulary.

Sure. What was a movie you saw recently, and what did you think of it?

I saw 'Silence of the Lambs' this week in English. It's a classic movie from years ago, but still very interesting to follow in English. The actors also spoke very clearly, which is sometimes a problem I find with American or British films.

Yes. And what kind of podcasts do you listen to?

There's one in particular called 'Going Global,' which is an American lady visiting lots of different countries and describing what she finds going on and the people there. Last week she was in Germany talking to people about their October festival, which apparently is a huge event there. That was interesting, because Germans seem to speak English amazingly well, almost like native speakers.

Thanks. Let's go on to Part 2 now. Please speak about this topic for one to two minutes, after preparing.

Part 2

Task card

Describe a typical day in your life at present
Say what you do
Say where you go and who you meet
Describe what you do with these people
And say if you think this will change in future

Candidate's notes during one minute preparation

Week day, waking up, going to work
My job, meetings, tasks, lunch, enjoyment, not WFH
After work: friends or home
May change, depends on relocation (USA)

Okay, please start speaking now.

I'm going to speak about a typical day for me, and I'll choose a week day rather than a weekend, because my week days are more varied and interesting. Generally speaking, my alarm goes off at seven am, but I make a point of not getting up right then. I like to put my headphones on and sometimes listen to some music, often some Brazilian or South African modern jazz which I like. At other times, I'll listen to a podcast on a subject that interests me, or possibly listen to the news on the BBC World Service. Around seven thirty I usually get up, and by eight am I'm having breakfast, which is usually some rolls, coffee and yoghurt. Most of the time at least one of my parents is still in the kitchen before going to work, so I have a chat with them about the day ahead and what time we'll see each other again. After that, I make sure I look reasonably presentable, then I go down to the street and get a tram from the corner of our block. By now I know a lot of people on the tram, the regulars as you might call them, and so we say hello to each other and have a little conversation. Then, by about eight forty-five, I'm usually at work.

I work for a company which makes tools and gadgets for camping, which means things you might need on a camp site for setting up your tent, cooking food and so on. I'm in the marketing department, which is an office with six people, and we're all at our desks by about nine am. Everybody says hello to each other, then we get on with our work. This means we go through our individual tasks, such as product design or budgeting, or alternatively we have group meetings about projects we're working on. There are usually at least two meetings during the day, sometimes three, and they last about an hour each. For example, this week we had a meeting about designing a new kind of multi-function camping knife, meaning we have to decide where it's going to be manufactured and how it's going to work. Another meeting was about how to build more of a relationship with our consumers, by making our online presence more interesting and useful for people going camping. These may sound like straightforward subjects, but once you start discussing them there's a huge amount of detail involved, and everybody wants to contribute one idea or another. The difficult aspect is often deciding which ideas to progress and which to leave behind, and, ultimately, it's the senior management who do that.

I tend to have lunch at about one or one thirty, and a group of us go to a café in the same street as the office. We all enjoy going for lunch together, and it's an inexpensive place to eat, so we tend to go there every day. I think we all enjoy the social side of having a meal together, because it builds up the rapport between us as a team and we can talk about things other than work. Our company has experimented with the idea of working from home, but none of us really wanted to do that, because we like going in to work and getting out of our home environments. I remember once that we were all working from home, and we agreed to go to our usual café and meet for lunch, which is quite funny if you think about it. After lunch, we all went into the office rather than back to our homes, because we felt we all worked better there and enjoyed it more. On a normal day, we wind up the office work at about six pm. After that, I sometimes meet with friends outside of work in the city. We all work in offices in the centre, so it's easy to meet up and do something relaxing. So we might go for a meal, for example, or maybe go bowling or to see a movie at the cinema. I do that once or twice a week, generally speaking, but not every night. If I don't go out in the city, I tend to go straight home and have a meal with my parents. We take it in turns to cook and set the table and so on. We often talk about chess, which is our shared interest, or the political events of the day. The discussions can get quite heated at times, as we all have different political views and we like to debate them. After dinner, sometimes we play a game of chess or we set out a chess board with a chess problem on it, and we talk about ways to make the next move and solve the problem. I'm usually asleep by midnight on a week day, because I need seven hours sleep at least, otherwise I feel exhausted the next day.

As for whether this will change in future, it certainly will if I move abroad and work for an American company, which is one possibility. If that happens, I'll be living in the USA and dealing with all the new aspects of life there, which I'm sure will be very different. But on the other hand, I may stay where I am, because I really enjoy it. If I do stay here, I'll stay with my current employer and just try to get promoted if I can. If that happens, my current routine probably won't change much at all.

(The candidate spoke for 1 minute 50 seconds.)

Thanks for that. Is this typical day very different from before you joined the company?

Yes, it's very different in some ways. I was at college before this, so I was studying all day, which didn't involve meetings or anything like that. On the other hand, I still get up and go to sleep at about the same time as before, so that hasn't changed.

Is there somewhere in particular you might live in the USA?

There's a very successful camping accessories company based in Delaware, so that's the one I'll try to join if I possibly can. The experience I've gained with my current firm would be ideal, but they have a lot of applicants and the visa process is complicated, so nothing's certain about the move at all.

I see. Now let's do Part 3, and we'll discuss how lifestyles are changing today.

Part 3

How are people's lifestyles changing at the moment?

Probably the biggest change, at least in this country, is the way people change jobs much more frequently during their lives. People are much less interested in conventional careers, meaning that someone might have four or five different jobs with different employers by the time they're thirty. Another change in lifestyle is the way that people dress much more informally at work, compared to the past. For instance, men don't often wear suits and ties to an office today, whereas only a few years ago they would have done so all the time. Away from work, another change is that young people commonly don't buy their own home until much later in life, because the cost of accommodation is so high. This means they have smaller families, or they don't have families at all, and so the birth rate goes down. These are all very noticeable changes, some minor but some really very important. I'm talking purely about this country, as I said at the start.

Yes. Are any of these changes positive?

I think the first two I mentioned are positive, yes. People are more creative and less stressed if they dress informally, and changing job frequently lets you gain more experience and skills more quickly. Compared to the old days of working in strict business clothes in the same job for twenty or twenty-five years, I think this is an improvement, because life must have been quite repetitive and boring back then. But the other point, about young people not being able to afford a home to live in, is very negative indeed. It means that people's whole lives are made more uncertain and less secure, which in turn causes a great deal of anxiety. That's very sad, and it reflects badly on our society in general, I think.

Thanks. What impact will Artificial Intelligence have on lifestyles in the future?

Well, there'll be many impacts from AI, even if we think about it in its current form, and not how it might change in the future. For one thing, it'll revolutionise studying and learning, because people will have this huge body of information available to them without having to research it themselves. Another change is that a large number of jobs will probably disappear, even in areas like law or finance, because AI can take over that kind of work and be functioning twenty-four hours instead of eight or nine hours a day. Apparently, a lot of young people are now reluctant to go into a career in accountancy, because they see the whole operation being done by AI in a few years. So, I'd say study and work are the areas of people's lives that will be affected most, and these are really huge changes that'll be very hard to cope with.

Do you think standards of living will be higher in the future?

It's difficult to say. On one side, you could say that, with technology improving all the time, people's lives will become more comfortable and convenient, and they'll have more opportunities for travel and leisure. But the problem is that people are under such economic pressure that it's hard to see how they'll be able to take advantage of these comforts, unless they're already very wealthy. As we just said, AI means that job opportunities will probably be more limited for many people, so they'll be less able to live such a relaxed lifestyle anyway. All in all, I don't think we can say that living standards will be higher in future, in fact. There's too much change and uncertainty involved.

Thanks, and that's the end of your test now.

***

Practice Test 20

Part 1

Let's talk about your friends and family. What do you like doing
with your friends?
How do you stay in touch with them?
Do you have any plans for the future with them?
What do your family do?
Do you live with your family? Where?

Part 2

Task card

Describe a journey you remember well
Say when this was and where you went
How you travelled and with who
What happened on the journey
And say what you did when you arrived

Examiner's follow up questions

Was the journey as you expected?
Have you kept in touch with anyone else involved?

Part 3

We'll discuss transport and making journeys
How can governments improve transport services?
How is the way people make journeys changing today?
Should cars be banned from cities? Why/why not?
How will city transport change in future?

***

Practice Test 20: Candidate's Page ✂

The examiner should cut this page from the book and give it to the candidate in Part 2, but not before

Part 2 Task card

Describe a journey you remember well
Say when this was and where you went
How you travelled and with who
What happened on the journey
And say what you did when you arrived

Space for Candidate to Make Notes in One-Minute Preparation Time

Band 9 Example Of Practice Test 20

Part 1

Let's talk about your friends firstly. What do you like doing with your friends?

Well, I live in a town with very limited scope for things to do in our free time. There are no cinemas or gyms, or any of the kind of facilities that larger towns have, unfortunately. That means we have to make our own entertainment, so we do things like fishing, cycling and hanging around in the main square, talking to friends. But, as you can imagine, it also means we spend a lot of time online, for something different to do.

How do you keep in touch with your friends?

I see them almost every day, because we all live near each other in the town. We've all grown up together, you see, and so we know each other very well. We also stay in touch online, so everyone always knows what everyone else is doing.

I see. What's your town like?

It's only a few thousand people, and, to be honest, it's a bit cut off from the rest of the world. Even to get to the nearest large town means a bus and then a train journey, unless I can borrow my dad's car. I do that sometimes, though, because I need a change of scene now and then.

Can you tell me more about your family? What do they do?

My father is a wholesaler in farming machinery, which is an important job in our area, so he's always very busy. My mother is a freelance journalist and she also works in his office, so it's a classic family business. I'm supposed to join them soon, actually, and work in the office too.

Would you like to do that?

I would, in the sense that it's a very interesting business and I already know quite a lot about it. But there again, I think I'd like to see a bit more of the outside world first, otherwise I won't have much experience outside our town.

What sort of plans do you have?

I'm thinking of moving to New Zealand for a year, to take an agricultural qualification there. They're experts at farming, obviously, and that would feed very well into my future work in the family firm at home. That's how I'm explaining it to my parents, anyway, and they're quite supportive of the idea.

Do you know people in New Zealand?

No, I don't, but I've heard that everyone's very friendly and it's easy to fit in. I know someone who went on vacation there once, and she says it's the most welcoming place she's ever been to. So I don't expect I'll get too homesick.

Do you live with your parents?

Yes, we have a large house where the ground floor is the machinery showroom and office, and upstairs is our family apartment. That's typical of family businesses in our area, because people literally live on top of their office or their workshop.

Yes. You said your mother was a journalist, what does she write?

She writes articles for a farming magazine, which are often reviews of new machines that farmers might use. She tests out every machine before it's sold, to find out its strengths and weaknesses.

What kind of machines do you sell?

Well, there are tractors and all the different attachments that go with them, I mean devices for digging or spreading stuff or ploughing up the ground. There are also machines for planting and harvesting, and some for pumping water for irrigation. Being in the family firm means we have to be experts on them all, so it's lucky I find it interesting.

Thanks for that. Now let's start Part 2, and here's your topic to speak about for one to two minutes after preparing for a minute.

Part 2

Task card

Describe a journey you remember well
Say when this was and where you went
How you travelled and with who
What happened on the journey
And say what you did when you arrived

Candidate's notes during one minute preparation

Visit to uncle in hospital, capital, with mum
Train (not plane) describe it, comfort, speed
Lunch, the bridge, the view both ways
Arrived, saw him, cousins, then return journey (storm)

Please start speaking now.

Okay, I'm going to speak about a journey I made a few years ago, when I was eighteen. The purpose of this journey was to go to the south of the country, near the capital city, where an uncle of mine was in hospital recovering from an illness. This was my mother's brother, so my mother was going to visit him and I went with her. We decided to go by train, because at the time there were a lot of delays and problems at the airports because of all the strikes that were happening. We thought it was better to have a slower journey by train than be forced to wait around in an airport for a long time. This turned out to be a sensible decision, because the airports went into absolute meltdown on the weekend that we left, and it was a good thing we'd pre-booked our train tickets. Everyone was trying to get onto the trains, so we were lucky in that respect. Well, my father drove my mum and myself to the city and saw us off at the station, and we boarded our train.

The train that we were booked onto was a high speed one, or at least high speed by our national standards. We don't have the real high speed trains like they do in Japan or France, but it was the type of modern train that travels fast and only stops at major cities. It was the first time I'd been on one of these, so I was very interested to see what it was like. I have to say it was very impressive. The seats were very large and comfortable, like the seat you get in premium class on a plane, except that they didn't recline. Our seats were next to the window, which made it feel even more like a plane. I remember that I sat opposite my mother, and there was a small table between us, and two very nice people got into the seats next to us. I'm often a bit anxious, to be honest, about who I end up sitting next to on a train or plane, because you're there for hours with them. But these two were very quiet, and they didn't try to engage us in a lengthy conversation, which sometimes happens. The cabin was air conditioned, and now and then a steward came round with a trolley of drinks, so it was really very relaxing.

It was a five-hour journey to the capital, and the time went by very quickly. We went pretty slowly out of the station, then we picked up a lot of speed in the countryside. We were going so fast that it was difficult to see much detail of what was going on close to the train, but if you looked further away you could see the fields and the hills in the background. I remember, at one point, a small plane started following us, but we were going so fast it looked like the pilot couldn't keep up with us, and in the end it fell behind. The thing I remember most, though, is that we went to the dining carriage for lunch, and the meal was excellent. It was almost like being in a good quality restaurant in a city, with stewards bring the dishes to the table and pouring the drinks for you and so on. Just as we were eating, the train went over a bridge which spans one of the big central valleys on the way to the capital, and the view as we went across the bridge was amazing. Through one window, we could see the valley with the river at the bottom, going all the way back to the central mountains on the horizon. Through the opposite window, there was the river spreading out into the delta that forms at that point, and on that horizon there was the ocean itself just about visible. It was a fascinating sight, but of course we only saw it for a few seconds before we left the bridge and went on overland. After lunch, we spent the time watching the view, chatting and listening to music on our earphones, which I enjoyed very much.

When we arrived in the capital, of course it was all very noisy and busy compared to what I'm used to at home. Fortunately, my uncle's sons, my cousins, met us at the station in their car. As it was only mid-afternoon, we went directly to the hospital to see my uncle. My cousins kept asking us if we were tired after the journey, but it had been such a relaxing time on the train that we didn't feel tired at all. So we saw my uncle, who was already getting better, and we stayed for a few days with my cousins, going into the hospital each day for a visit. Finally, we went home again on the same train, of course, and once again the journey was great. The difference was that there was a huge storm and torrential rain, so we didn't get much of a view on the way home.

(The candidate spoke for 1 minute 45 seconds.)

Thanks for that. I hope your uncle recovered fully?

He did, thanks, and he's completely back to normal now. It was a good chance to see him and also to catch up with my cousins, who I hadn't seen for ages.

Was the train itself what you expected?

It was better than I expected, definitely. I'd seen pictures, but I wasn't expecting it to be so comfortable compared to the normal trains, which can be quite basic, as I'm sure you know. And the quality of the lunch service was a huge surprise. I put a review online, in fact, and I gave it five stars, because it certainly deserved it.

Thanks, and now we come to Part 3, and we'll discuss transport generally.

Part 3

How do you think governments can improve transport services?

In several ways, I think. For one thing, they can make sure the basic infrastructure for transport is in good condition, for example the roads and the rail lines themselves. Most people would agree that's one of the fundamental tasks of a government. Another thing they can do is to subsidise the cost of using transport, so that ticket prices aren't so excessively high that people can't afford to travel anywhere. Oh, and there's another role for the government to play in developing new forms of transport, for example with alternatives to oil-based fuels. We need state resources to do research in those areas, because of the enormous costs. So, I'd say infrastructure, subsidy and research, those three things are the key points.

Thanks. Should cars be banned from cities?

It's a difficult question to answer. Some people would say that cars are dangerous and polluting, and even electric cars should be excluded because that would free up the streets for pedestrians. But another view is that, if you stopped people using private cars, city centres would soon become empty as everyone stayed away. For example, there are cities in Britain that have excluded cars, and they've found that lots of businesses have to close down because there aren't enough customers coming in. All in all, I wouldn't ban cars completely, because of that kind of evidence. There's no point having a car free city if everything is closed.

Thanks. How will city transport change in future, maybe?

What's the future of transport in cities? Well, we might see public rail transport even in smaller cities that don't have a metro-type system today. As lines can be built much more easily than in the past, and the trains themselves are much lighter and quieter, even smaller towns could have a local metro system. Another change could be pay-as-you-go car use, where you pay a subscription to have a car only when you need it, not all the time. That way, there are fewer cars around, but they're still available when you want one. One thing we'll definitely see is more pedestrian vehicles such as e-scooters and personal boards, so people can get around much more quickly than by walking, but without needing a bus. These are all quite exciting developments.

I see. How is the way people make journeys changing today?

Probably the biggest change is the use of non-fossil fuels for engines, such as hydrogen or biofuel, and of course electric vehicles becoming more widespread. Electric power is being used for bikes and e-scooters too, which people didn't have until quite recently. All this makes people's journeys generally less polluting. Another change is that people today are much more aware of the environmental impact of any journey they make, so they often decide whether to travel or not based on that factor. And if they do decide to travel, they'll often try to minimise the footprint they create, for instance by choosing a transport company that offsets its carbon or something similar. So new fuels and more awareness, those are the big changes I can see.

Thanks. We've finished your test now.

***

More Help From the Experts

You've now finished Book 1 in our series on IELTS speaking, and you should now be much better prepared for the test than before you started. You should now have a strong command of how to approach each part of the test, and how to structure your answers in each part. For continued practice, Book 2 in this series (ISBN 979-8335257527) contains a further twenty complete practice tests, together with band 9 transcripts and vocab builder sections to develop your vocabulary even further.

If you're taking IELTS, you'll also need to prepare for Task 2 of the Writing Test, which is the same for both Academic and General Training tests. We have a range of advice books to help you with this and maximise your score.

If you're taking the General Training test, we also have a book on how to write the letters in your GT Task 1 writing.

Please search 'Amazon Cambridge IELTS Consultants' to see our full range of IELTS books.

cambridgeielts@outlook.com

Made in the USA
Columbia, SC
23 June 2025